A Novelist on Novels by W. L. George

Walter Lionel George was born to British parents on 20th March 1882 in Paris, France.

It was not until he was a young man of 20 that he learned English. In 1905 he moved to London to work in an office but soon found himself working as a journalist, as a foreign correspondent, for various London newspapers.

By 1911, with the publication of his first novel 'A Bed of Roses', which portrayed the fall of a penniless young woman into prostitution, his efforts were rewarded and he turned to literature as a full time career.

His writings now sold well. He added short stories to his offerings as well as literary essays and several tracts that discussed left-wing themes. Others thought his subject matter to be difficult and poorly chosen and his political views gained him little credit amongst his peers although such luminaries as George Orwell praised both subject matter and style.

His personal life was also turbulent. His three marriages left him widowed twice. In 1908 he married Helen Porter who died in 1914, Helen Agnes Moorhead followed in 1916 but she died in 1920. His last marriage was to Kathleen Geipel in 1921.

W. L George died on 30th January 1926.

I0163629

Index of Contents

A Deceptive Dedication

I

I have shown the manuscript of this book to a well-known author. One of those staid, established authors whose venom has been extracted by the mellow years. My author is beyond rancour and exploit; he has earned the right to bask in his own celebrity, and needs to judge no more, because no longer does he fear judgment. He is like a motorist who has sowed his wild petrol. He said to me: 'You are very, very unwise. I never criticise my contemporaries, and, believe me, it doesn't pay.' Well, I am unwise; I always was unwise, and this has paid in a coin not always recognised, but precious to a man's spiritual pride. Why should I not criticise my contemporaries? It is not a merit to be a contemporary. Also, they can return the compliment; some of them, if I may venture upon a turn of phrase proper for Mr Tim Healy, have returned the compliment before they got it. It may be unwise, but I join with Voltaire in thanking God that he gave us folly. So I will affront the condemnatory vagueness of wool and fleecy cloud, be content to think that nobody will care where I praise, that everybody will think me impertinent where I judge. I will be content to believe that the well-known author will not mind if I criticise him, and that the others will not mind either. I will hope, though something of a Sadducee, that there is an angel in their hearts.

I want to criticise them and their works because I think the novel, this latest born of literature, immensely interesting and important. It is interesting because, more faithfully than any other form, it expresses the mind of man, his pains that pass, his hopes that fade and are born again, his discontent pregnant with energy, the unrulinesses in which he misspends his vigour, the patiences that fit him to endure all things even though he dare them not. In this, all other forms fail: history, because it chronicles battles and dates, yet not the great movements of the peoples; economics, because in their view all men are vile; biography, because it leads the victim to the altar, but never sacrifices it. Even poetry fails; I do not try to shock, but I doubt whether the poetic is equal to the prose form.

I do not want to fall into the popular fallacy that prose and poetry each have their own field, strictly preserved, for prose is not always prosy, nor poetry always poetic; prose may contain poetry, poetry cannot contain prose, just as some gentlemen are bounders, but no bounders are gentlemen. But the admiration many people feel for poetry derives from a lack of intelligence rather than from an excess of emotion, and they would be cured if, instead of admiring, they read. Some subjects and ideas naturally fall into poetry, mainly the lyric ideas; 'To Anthea,' and 'The Skylark' would, in prose, lie broken-pinioned upon the ground, but the exquisiteness of poetry, when it conveys the ultimate aspiration of man, defines its limitations. Poetry is child of the austerity of literature by the sensuality of music. Thus it is more and less than its forbears; speaking for myself alone, I feel that 'Epipsychidion' and the 'Grecian Urn' are just a little less than the Kreutzer Sonata, that Browning and Whitman might have written better in prose, though they might thus have been less quoted. For poetry is too often schwaermerei, a thing of lilts; when it conveys philosophical ideas, as in Browning and in that prose writer gone astray, Shakespeare, it suffers the agonising pains of constriction. Rhyme and scansion tend to limit and hamper it; everything can be said in prose, but not in poetry; to prose no licence need be granted, while poetry must use and abuse it, for prose is free, poetry shackled by its form. No doubt that is why poetry causes so much stir, for it surmounts extraordinary difficulties, and men gape as at a tenor who attains a top note. However exquisite, the scope of poetry is smaller than that of prose, and if any doubt it let him open at random an English Bible and say if Milton can out-thunder Job, or Swinburne outcloy the sweetness of Solomon's Song.

More than interesting, the novel is important because, low as its status may be, it does day by day express mankind, and mankind in the making. Sometimes it is the architect that places yet another brick upon the palace of the future. Always it is the showman of life. I think of 'serious books,' of the incredible heaps of memoirs, works on finance, strategy, psychology, sociology, biology, omniology ... that fall every day like manna (unless from another region they rise as fumes) into the baskets of the reviewers. All this paper ... they dance their little dance to four hundred readers and a great number of second-hand booksellers, and lo! the dust of their decay is on their brow. They live a little longer than an article by Mr T. P. O'Connor, and live a little less.

The novel, too, does not live long, but I have known one break up a happy home, and another teach revolt to several daughters; can we give greater praise? Has so much been achieved by any work entitled The Foundations of the Century, or something of that sort? The novel, despised buffoon that it is, pours out its poison and its pearls within reach of every lip; its heroes and heroines offer examples to the reader and make him say: 'That bold, bad man ... you wouldn't think it to look at me, who'm a linen-draper, but it's me.' If, in this preface, I may introduce a personal reminiscence, I can strengthen my point by saying that after publishing The Second Blooming I received five letters from women I did not know, who wholly recognised themselves in my principal heroine, of course the regrettable one.

The novel moulds by precept and example, and therefore we modern jesters, inky troubadours, are responsible for the gray power which we wield behind the throne. Given this responsibility, it is a pity there should be so many novels, for the reader is distracted with various examples, and painfully hesitates between the career of Raffles and that of John Inglesant. Thus the novel fires many a sanctimoniousness, makes lurid many a hesitating life. If only we could endow it! But we cannot, for the old saying can be garbled: call no novelist famous until he is dead.

It is a fascinating idea, this one of endowing the novel. In principle it is not difficult, only we must assume our capable committee and that is quite as difficult as ignoring the weight of the elephant. I wonder what would happen if an Act of Parliament were to endow genius! I wonder who would sit on the sub-committee appointed by the British Government to endow literature. I do not wonder, I know. There would be Professor Saintsbury, Mr Austin Dobson, Professor Walter Raleigh, Sir Sidney Lee, Professor Gollancz, all the academics, all the people drier than the drought, who, whether the god of literature find himself in the car or in the cart, never fail to get into the dickey. I should not even wonder if, by request of the municipality of Burton-on-Trent, it were found desirable to infuse a democratic element into the sub-committee by adding the manager of the Army and Navy Stores and, of course, Mr Bottomley. Do not protest: Mr Bottomley has recently passed embittered judgments, under the characteristic heading 'Dam-Nation,' on Mr Alec Waugh, who ventured, in a literary sketch, to show English soldiers going over the top with oaths upon their lips and the courage born of fear in their hearts. I think Mr Bottomley would like to have Mr Waugh shot, and the editor of The Nation confined for seven days in the Press Bureau, for having told the truth in literary form. I do not impugn his judgment of what it feels like to go over the top, for he has had long experience of keeping strictly on the surface.

No, our sub-committee would be appointed without the help of Thalia and Calliope. It would register judgments such as those of the famous sub-committee that grants the Nobel Prizes. That committee, during its short life, has managed to reward Sully-Prudhomme and to leave out Swinburne, to give a prize to Sienkewicz, whom a rather more recent generation has found so suitable for the cinema. It has even given a prize to Mr Rudyard Kipling, but whether in memory of literature or dynamite is not known.

So literary genius must, as before, look for its endowment in the somewhat barren heart of man, and continue to shed a hundred seeds in its stony places, in the forlorn hope that the fowls of the air may not devour them all, and that a single ear of corn may wilt and wither its way into another dawn.

II

The reading of most men and women provides distressing lists. So far as I can gather from his conversation, the ordinary, busy man, concerned with his work, finds his mental sustenance in the newspapers, particularly in Punch, in the illustrated weeklies and in the journals that deal with his trade; as for imaginative literature, he seems to confine himself to Mr Nat Gould, Sir Arthur Conan Doyle, Mr W. W. Jacobs, Mr Mason, and such like, who certainly do not strain his imaginative powers; he is greatly addicted to humour of the coarser kind, and he dissipates many of his complexes by means of vile stories which he exchanges with his fellows; these do not at all represent his kindliness and his respectability. Sometimes he reads a shocker, the sort that is known as 'railway literature,' presumably because it cannot hold the attention for more than the time that elapses between two stops.

The more serious and scholarly man, who abounds in every club, is addicted to the monthly reviews, (price two-and-six; he does not like the shilling ones), to the Times, to the Spectator; that kind of man is definitely stodgy and prides himself upon being sound. He is fond of memoirs, rather sodden accounts of aristocrats and politicians, of the dull, ordinary lives of dull, ordinary people; when he has done with the book it goes to the pulping machine, but some of the pulp gets into that man's brain. ('Ashes to ashes, pulp to pulp.') He likes books of travel, biographies, solid French books (strictly by academicians), political works, economic works. His conversation sounds like it, and that is why his wife is so bored; his emotions are reflex and run only round the objects he can see; art cannot touch him, and no feather ever falls upon his brow from an airy wing. He commonly tells you that good novels are not written nowadays; he must be excused that opinion, for he never tries to read them. The only novels with which the weary Titan refreshes his mind are those of Thackeray, sometimes of Trollope; the more frivolous sometimes go so far as to sip a little of the honey that falls from the mellifluous lips of Mr A. C. Benson.

The condition of women is different. They care for little that ends in 'ic,' and so their consumption of novels is enormous. The commonplace woman is attracted by the illustrated dailies and weeklies, but she also needs large and continuous doses of religious sentimentality, of papier maché romance, briefly, of novels described in literary circles as 'bilge,' such as the works of Mr Hall Caine, Mrs Barclay, Miss E. M. Dell, and a great many more; if she is of the slightly faster kind that gives smart lunch parties at the Strand Corner House, her diet is sometimes a little stronger; she takes to novels of the orchid house and the tiger's lair, to the artless erotics of Miss Elinor Glyn, Mr Hubert Wales, and Miss Victoria Cross. She likes memoirs too, memoirs of vague Bourbons and salacious Bonapartes; she takes great pleasure in the historical irregularities of cardinals. She likes poetry too as conveyed by Miss Ella Wheeler Wilcox.

If that type of woman were not a woman the arts could base as few hopes on her as they do on men, but the most stupid woman is better ground than the average man, because she is open, while he is smug. So it is no wonder that among the millions of women who mess and muddle their way through the conservatories and pigsties of literature, should be found the true reading public, the women who are worth writing for, who read the best English novels, who are in touch with French and Russian literature, who reads plays, and even essays, ancient and modern. Hail Mary, mother of mankind; but for these the arts must starve!

That fine public cannot carry us very far. They are not enough to keep literature vigorous by giving it what it needs: a consciousness of fellowship with many readers. If literature is to flourish (of which I am not sure, though endure in some form it will), the general public taste must be raised. I feel that taste can be raised and cultivated, and many have felt that too. From the middle of the nineteenth century onwards, and especially since 1870, an ascending effort has been made to stimulate the taste of the rising artisan. Books like Lord Avebury's Pleasures of Life, like Sesame and Lilies, collections such as the Hundred Best Books and the Hundred Best Pictures, have all been attuned to that key. The only pity is that the selections, nearly all of them excellent, were immeasurably above the heads of the public for which they were meant. Two recent instances are worth analysing. One of them is A Library for Five Pounds by Sir William Robertson Nicoll, (whom Mr Arnold Bennett delighteth to revile), the other Literary Taste and How to Form It, by Mr Bennett himself. Now Sir William Robertson Nicoll's book is much more sensible than the funereal lists available at most polytechnics. The author does not pretend that one should read Plato in one's bath; he seems to realise the state of mind of the ordinary, fairly busy, fairly willing, fairly intelligent person. A sign of it is that he selects only sixty-one works, and out of those allows twenty-seven novels. Of the rest, most are readable, except Pilgrim's Progress and The Origin of Species, a touching couple. The list is by far the best guide I have ever seen, but ... there is not a living author in it. It is not a library, it is a necropolis. The novelists that Sir William Robertson Nicoll recommends are Scott, Jane Austen, Dickens, Thackeray, Charlotte Brontë, George Eliot, Hawthorne, Trollope, Blackmore, Defoe, and Swift. All their books are readable, but they do not take by the hand the person who has thought wrong or not thought at all. When you want to teach a child history you do not dump upon its desk Hume and Smollett, in forty volumes; you lead it by degrees, by means of text-books, that is according to plan. That is how I conceive literary education, but before suggesting a list, let us glance at Literary Taste and How to Form It. In this book the author shows himself much more unpractical and much less sympathetic than Sir William Robertson Nicoll (whom Mr Bennett delighteth to revile). The book itself is very interesting; it is bright, intelligent; it teaches you how to read, and how to make allowances for the classics; it tells you how you may woo your way to Milton, but, after all, when you have done, you find that you have not wooed your way an inch nearer. That is because Mr Arnold Bennett takes up to his public an attitude more highbrowed than I could imagine if I were writing a skit on his book. Mr Bennett's idea of a list for the aspirant to letters is to throw the London Library at his head; he lays before us a stodgy lump of two or three hundred volumes, many of them excellent, and many more absolutely penal. It is enough to say that he seriously starts his list with the Venerable Bede's Ecclesiastical History. Bede! the dimmest, most distant of English chroniclers, who depicts the dimmest and most distant period of English history; once, in an A.B.C., I saw a shopman reading Tono-Bungay, which was propped against the cruet. Does Mr Bennett imagine that man dropping the tear of emotion and the gravy of excitement upon the Venerable Bede? And if one goes on with the list and discovers the Autobiography of Lord Herbert of Cherbury, Religio Medici, Berkeley's Principles of Human Knowledge, Reynold's Discourses on Art, the works of Pope, Voyage of the Beagle ... one comes to understand how such readers may have been made by such masters. From the beginning to the end of that list my mind is obsessed by the word 'stodge,' and the novels do not relieve it much. There are a good many, but they comprise the usual Thackeray, Scott, Dickens ... need I go on? Relief is found only in Fielding, Sterne, and in one book each of Marryat, Lever, Kingsley, and Gissing. These authors are admitted presumably because they are dead.

In all this, where is hope? How many green daffodil heads, trying to burst their painful way through the heavy earth of a dull life, has Mr Bennett trampled on? Is it impossible to find some one who is (as Mr Bennett certainly is), capable of the highest artistic appreciation and of high literary achievement, and who will, for a moment, put himself in the place of the people he is addressing? Is it impossible for an adult to remember that as a boy he hated the classics? Has he forgotten that as a young man he could be charmed, but educated only by means of a machine like the one they use for stuffing geese? The people we want to introduce to literature are, nearly all of them, people who work; some earn thirty shillings a week, and ponder a great deal on how to live on it; some earn hundreds a year and are not much better off; all are occupied with material cares, their work, their games, their gardens, their loves; nearly all are short of time, and expend on work, transit, and meals, ten to twelve hours a day. They read in tubes and omnibuses, in the midst of awful disturbance and overcrowding; also they are deeply corrupted by the daily papers, where nothing over a column is ever printed, where the news are conveyed in paragraphs and headlines, so that they never have to concentrate, and find it difficult to do so; they are corrupted too by the vulgarity and sensationalism which are the bones and blood of the magazines, until they become unable to think without stimulants.

It is no use saying those people are lost. They are not lost, but they have gone astray, or rather, nobody has ever tried to turn their faces the right way. Certainly Mr Arnold Bennett does nothing for them. If they could read The Decline and Fall of the Roman Empire they would, but they cannot. People cannot plunge into old language, old atmospheres; they have no links with these things; their imagination is not trained to take a leap; many try, and nearly all fail because their literary leaders go to sleep, or march them into bogs. No crude mind can jump into ancient literature; modern literature alone can help it, namely cleanse its nearest section, and prepare it for further strain. The limits of literary taste can, in each person, be carried as far as that person's intellectual capacity goes, but only by degrees. In other words, limit your objective instead of failing at a large operation.

I am not prepared to lay down a complete list, but I am prepared to hint at one. If I had to help a crude but willing taste, I would handle its reading as follows:—

FIRST PERIOD

Reading made up exclusively of recent novels, good, well-written, thoughtful novels, not too startling in form or contents. I would begin on novels because anybody can read a novel, and because the first cleansing operation is to induce the subject to read good novels instead of bad ones. Here is a preliminary list:—

Tony-Bungay (Wells) Kipps (Wells) The Custom of the Country (Wharton) The Old Wives' Tale (Bennett) The Man of Property (Galsworthy) Jude the Obscure (Hardy) Tess of the D'Urbervilles (Hardy) Sussex Gorse (Kaye-Smith)

and say twenty or thirty more of this type, all published in the last dozen years. It is, of course, assumed that interest would be maintained by conversation.

SECOND PERIOD

After the subject (victim, if you like) had read say thirty of the best solid novels of the twentieth century, I think I should draw him to the more abstruse modern novels and stories. In the first period he would come in contact with a general criticism of life. In the second period he would read novels of a more iconoclastic and constructive kind, such as:—

The Island Pharisees (Galsworthy) The New Machiavelli (Wells) Sinister Street (Mackenzie) The Celestial Omnibus (Forster) The Longest Journey (Forster) Sons and Lovers (Lawrence) The White Peacock (Lawrence) Ethan Frome (Wharton) Round the Corner (Cannan)

Briefly, the more ambitious kind of novel, say thirty or forty altogether. At that time, I should induce the subject to browse occasionally in the Oxford Book of English Verse.

THIRD PERIOD

Now only would I come to the older novels, because, by then, the mind should be supple enough to stand their congestion of detail, their tendency to caricature, their stilted phrasing, and yet recognise their qualities. Here are some:—

The Rise of Silas Lapham (Howells) Vanity Fair (Thackeray) The Vicar of Wakefield (Goldsmith) The Way of All Flesh (Butler) Quentin Durward (Scott) Guy Mannering (Scott)

Briefly, the bulk of the works of Thackeray, Jane Austen, Charlotte Brontë, and George Eliot. 'Barry Lyndon' twice, and Trollope never. Here, at last, the solid curriculum, but only, you will observe, when a little of the mud of the magazines had been cleaned off. Rather more verse too, beginning with Tennyson and Henley, passing on to Rossetti and perhaps to Swinburne. Verse, however, should not be pressed. But I think I should propose modern plays of the lighter kind, Mr Bernard Shaw's Major Barbara and John Bull's Other Island, for instance. One could pass by degrees to the less obvious plays of Mr Shaw, certainly to those of St John Hankin, and perhaps to The Madras House. I think also a start might be made on foreign works, but these would develop mainly in the

FOURTH PERIOD

Good translations being available, I would suggest notably:—

Madame Bovary (Flaubert) Resurrection (Tolstoi) Fathers and Children (Turgenev) Various short stories of Tchekoff.

And then, if the subject seemed to enjoy these works,

L'Education Sentimentale (Flaubert) Le Rouge et le Noir (Stendhal) The Brothers Karamazov (Dostoievsky)

Mark this well, if the subject seemed to enjoy them. If there is any strain, any boredom, there is lack of continuity, and a chance of losing the subject's interest altogether. I think the motto should be 'Don't press'; that is accepted when it comes to golf; why has it never been accepted when it affects man? This period would, I think, end with the lighter plays of Shakespeare, such as The Merry Wives of Windsor, The Taming of the Shrew, and perhaps Hamlet. I think modern essays should also come in via Mr E. V. Lucas, Mr Belloc, and Mr Street; also I would suggest Synge's travels in Wicklow, Connemara, and the Arran Islands; this would counteract the excessive fictional quality of the foregoing.

FIFTH PERIOD

I submit that, by that time, if the subject had a good average mind, he would be prepared by habit to read older works related with the best modern works. The essays of Mr Lucas would prepare him for the works of Lamb; those of Mr Belloc, for the essays of Carlyle and Bacon. Thus would I lead back to the heavier Victorian novels, to the older ones of Fielding and Sterne. If any taste for plays has been developed by Shakespeare, it might be turned to Marlowe, Congreve, and Sheridan. The drift of my argument is: read the easiest first; do not strain; do not try to 'improve your mind,' but try to enjoy yourself. Than books there is no better company, but it is no use approaching them as dour pedagogues. Proceed as a snob climbing the social ladder, namely, know the best people in the neighbourhood, then the best people they know. The end is not that of snobbery, but an eternal treasure.

I think that my subject, if capable of developing taste, would find his way to the easier classic works, such as Carlyle's French Revolution, Boswell's Life of Johnson, perhaps even to Wesley's Journal. But at that stage the subject would have to be dismissed to live or die. Enough would have been done to lead him away from boredom, from dull solemnity and false training, to purify his taste and make it of some use. The day is light and the past is dark; all eyes can see the day and find it splendid, but eyes that would pierce the darkness of the past must grow familiar with lighter mists; to every man the life of the world about him is that man's youth, while old age is ill to apprehend.

Litany of the Novelist

I

There are times when one wearies of literature; when one reads over one's first book, reflects how good it was, and how greatly one was misunderstood; when one considers the perils and misadventures of so accidental a life and likens oneself to those dogs described by Pliny who run fast as they drink from the Nile for fear they should be seized by the crocodiles; when one tires of following Mr Ford Madox Hueffer's advice, 'to sit down in the back garden with pen, ink, and paper, to put vine leaves in one's hair and to write'; when one remembers that in Flaubert's view the literary man's was a dog's life (metaphors about authors lead you back to the dog) but that none other was worth living. In those moods, one does not agree with Flaubert; rather, one agrees with Butler:—

'... those that write in rhyme still make The one verse for the other's sake; For one for sense and one for rhyme, I think's sufficient at one time.'

One sees life like Mr Polly, as 'a rotten, beastly thing.' One sighs for adventure, to become a tramp or an expert witness. One knows that one will never be so popular as Beecham's pills; thence is but a step to picture oneself as less worthy.

We novelists are the showmen of life. We hold up its mirror, and, if it look at us at all, it mostly makes faces at us. Indeed a writer might have with impunity sliced Medusa's head: she would never have noticed him. The truth is that the novelist is a despised creature. At moments, when, say, a learned professor has devoted five columns to showing that a particular novelist is one of the pests of society, the writer feels exalted. But as society shows no signs of wanting to be rid of the pest, the novelist begins to doubt his own pestilency. He is wrong. In a way, society knows of our existence, but does not worry; it shows this in a curiously large number of ways, more than can be enumerated here. It sees the novelist as a man apart; as a creature fraught with venom, and, paradoxically, a creature of singularly lamb-like and unpractical temperament.

Consider, indeed, the painful position of a respectable family whose sons make for Threadneedle Street every day, its daughters for Bond Street and fashion, or for the East End, good works, and social advancement. Imagine that family, who enjoys a steady income, shall we say in the neighbourhood of £5000 a year, enough to keep it in modest comfort, confronted with the sudden infatuation of one of its daughters for an unnamed person, met presumably in the East End where he was collecting copy. You can imagine the conversation after dinner:—

Angeline: 'What does he do, father? Oh, well! he's a novelist.'

Father: .... What! a novelist! One of those long-haired, sloppy-collared ragamuffins without any soles to their boots! Do you think that because I've given you a motor-car I'm going to treat you to a husband? A bar loafer ... (we are always intemperate) ... A man whom your mother and sisters ... (our morals are atrocious) ... I should not wonder if the police ... (we are all dishonest, and yet we never have any money) ... I was talking to the Bishop ... (we practise no religion, except that occasionally we are Mormons)....

And so on, and so on. Father won't have it, and if in the end Father does have it he finds that Angeline's eyes are not blacked, but that Angeline's husband's boots are blacked, that the wretched fellow keeps a balance at the bank, can ride a horse, push a perambulator, drive a nail; but he does not believe it for a long time. For it is, if not against all experience, at any rate against all theory that a novelist should be eligible. The bank clerk is eligible, the novelist is not; we are not 'safe,' we are adventurers, we have theories, and sometimes the audacity to live up to them. We are often poor, which happens to other men, and this is always our own fault, while it is often their misfortune. Of late years, we have grown still more respectable than our forefathers, who were painfully such: Dickens lived comfortably in Marylebone; Thackeray reigned in a luxurious house near Kensington Square and in several first-class clubs; Walter Scott reached a terrible extreme of respectability; he went bankrupt, but later on paid his debts in full. Yet we never seem quite respectable, perhaps because respectability is so thin a varnish. Even the unfortunate girls whom we 'entice away from good homes' into the squalor of the arts, do not think us respectable. For them half the thrill of marrying a novelist consists in the horror of the family which must receive him; it is like marrying a quicksand, and the idea is so bitter that a novelist who wears his hair long might do well to marry a girl who wears hers short. He will not find her in the bourgeoisie.

The novelist is despised because he produces a commodity not recognised as 'useful.' There is no definition of usefulness, yet everybody is clear that the butcher, the railway porter, the stock jobber are useful; that they fulfil a function necessary for the maintenance of the State. The pugilist, the dancer, the music hall actor, the novelist, produce nothing material, while the butcher does. To live, one wants meat, but not novels. We need not pursue this too far and ask the solid classes to imagine a world without arts, presumably they could not. It is enough to point the difference, and to suggest that we are deeply enthralled by the Puritan tradition which calls pleasure, if not noxious, at any rate unimportant; the maintenance of life is looked upon as more essential than the enjoyment thereof, so that many people picture an ideal world as a spreading cornfield dotted with cities that pay good rents, connected by railways which pay good dividends. They resemble the revolutionary, who on the steps of the guillotine said to Lavoisier: 'La Republique n'a pas besoin de savants.' This is obvious when the average man (which includes many women) alludes to the personality of some well-known writer. One he has come to respect: Mr Hall Caine, because popular report says that his latest novel brought him in about a hundred thousand pounds, but those such as Mr Arnold Bennett and Mr H. G. Wells leave strange shadows upon his memory. Of Mr Bennett he says: 'Oh, yes, he writes about the North Country, doesn't he? Or is it the West Country? Tried one of his books once. I forget its name, and now I come to think of it, it may have been by somebody else. He must be a dreary sort of chap, anyhow, sort of methodist.'

Mr H. G. Wells is more clearly pictured: 'Wells? the fellow who writes about flying machines and men in the moon. Jules Verne sort of stuff, isn't it? He's a Socialist.'

And so out with Mr Bennett, one of our best modern stylists, who in spite of an occasional crowding of the canvas has somehow fixed for us the singular and ferocious tribe from which he springs; so out with Mr Wells, with his restless, impulsive, combative, infinitely audacious mind. The average man says: 'Flying machines,' and the passion of Mr Wells for a beautiful, if somewhat over-hygienic world is swept away. Those are leading instances. Others, such as Mr Conrad, Miss Edith Wharton, O. Henry, Mr Galsworthy, are not mentioned at all; if the name of Mr Henry James is spoken, it leads up to a gibe at long sentences.

The attitude is simple; we are not taken seriously. Novelists have to take mankind seriously because they want to understand it; mankind is exempt from the obligation because it does not conceive the desire. We are not people who take degrees, who can be scheduled and classified. We are not Doctors of Science, Licentiates of Music Schools. We are just men and women of some slight independence, therefore criminals, men who want to observe and not men who want to do, therefore incredible. And so, because we cannot fall into the classes made for those who can be classified, we are outside class, below class. We are the mistletoe on the social oak.

It is perhaps in search of dignity and status that the modern novelist has taken to journalism. Journalism raises a novelist's status, for a view expressed by a fictitious character is not taken seriously, while the same view fastened to an event of the day acquires importance, satisfies the specific function of the press, which is more and more that of a champion of found causes. The newspaper is a better jumping-off ground than the pulpit or the professorial chair; it enjoys a vast circulation, which the novel does not; it conveys an idea to millions of people who would never think of buying a newspaper for the sake of an idea, but who buy it for news, murder cases or corn market reports; it is a place where a writer may be serious, because the newspaper is labelled as serious, while the novel is labelled as frivolous.

This is vital to the proposition, and explains why so many novelists have sought refuge in the press. It is not exactly a question of money. Journalism rewards a successful novelist better than does the novel, though successful novelists make very good incomes; they often earn as much as the red-nosed comedian with the baggy trousers and the battered bowler. Thackeray, Washington Irving, Kingsley, and notably Dickens, knew the value of journalism. Dickens was the most peculiar case, for it is fairly clear that Nicholas Nickleby helped to suppress the ragged schools and that Oliver Twist was instrumental in reforming workhouse law; both works were immensely successful, but Dickens felt that he wanted a platform where he could be always wholly serious: for this the Daily News was born in 1846. Likewise Mr Wells has written enormously upon the war and economics; Mr Arnold Bennett has printed many political articles; Mr Galsworthy has become more direct than a novelist can be and written largely on cruelty to animals, prison reform, etc. It is the only way in which we can be taken seriously. We must be solemn, a little dull, patriotic or unpatriotic, socialistic or conservative; there is only one thing we may not be, and that is creative and emotional.

It should be said in passing that even the press does not think much of us. Articles on solid subjects by novelists are printed, well paid for, sought after; it does a paper good to have an article on Imperial Federation by Mr Kipling, or on Feminism by Mr Zangwill. The novelist amounts to a poster; he is a blatant advertisement; he is a curiosity, the man who makes the public say: 'I wonder what the Daily — is up to now.' Be assured that Mr Zangwill's views on Feminism do not command the respectful treatment that is accorded a column leader in the Times; he is too human; he sparkles too much; he has not the matchless quality of those leaders which compels you to put on an extra stamp if you have to send the paper through the post.

The newspapers court the novelist as the people of a small town court the local rich man, but neither newspaper nor little town likes very much the object of its courtship. Except when they pay us to express them, the newspapers resent our having any views at all; the thought behind is always: 'Why can't the fellows mind their own business, and go on writing about love and all that sort of stuff?' During the war, references to novelists who express their views have invariably been sneering; it is assumed that because we are novelists we are unable to comprehend tactics, politics, in fact any 'ics,' except perhaps the entirely unimportant aesthetics. But the peculiarity of the situation is that not a voice has been raised against professors of philology, who write on finance, against Bishops dealing with land settlement, against doctors when they re-map Europe, against barristers, businessmen.... These may say anything they like; they are plain, hard-headed men, while our heads are soft enough to admit a new idea.

To define the attitude of the press is in modern times to define the attitude of the State. From our point of view this is frigid. In America, there are no means of gauging a novelist's position, for American classification rests upon celebrity and fortune. Ours rests upon breeding and reliability. America is more adventurous; Britannia rides in a chariot, while the American national emblem foreshadowed the aeroplane. And so, in the United States it may profit a man as well to be a Jack London as an Elihu Root. America has no means of recognising status, while in England we have honours. We distribute a great many honours, and indeed the time may come, as Mr Max Beerbohm says, when everybody will be sentenced to a knighthood without the option of a fine. Honours are rather foolish things, monuments that create a need for circumspection; they are often given for merits not easily perceived, but still they are a rough test of status. Setting aside money, which is the primary qualification, and justifies Racine in saying that without money honour is nothing but a disease, a title is a fairly clear sign of distinction. Sir Edward Shackleton, Sir Douglas Haig, Sir Frederick Treves, Lord Reading, Sir William Crookes, Lord Lister, all those titles are obvious recognition of prominence in Polar Exploration, the Army, the Law, Medicine, Research, as the case may be; there are scores of Medical Knights, many Law Lords, many Major Generals and Admirals endowed with the Knight Commandership of the Bath. We do not complain. They deserve their honours, most of them. They deserve them more than the politicians who have received for long service rewards that ability could not give them, than the Lord Mayors who are titled because they sold, for instance, large quantities of kitchen fenders. When we consider the arts, we observe a discrepancy. The arts do not ask for honours; they are too arrogant, and know that born knights cannot be knighted. Only they claim that an attempt should be made to honour them, to grant them Mr Gladstone's and Mr Chamberlain's privilege of refusing honours.

Consider, for instance, the Order of Merit, one of the highest honours that the British Crown can confer. At the end of last year it numbered twenty-one members. Among them were some distinguished foreigners, Prince Oyama, Prince Yamagata and Admiral Togo; historians, pro-consuls, four Admirals ... and one novelist. Mr Thomas Hardy. We do not complain that only Mr Thomas Hardy was chosen, for there is nobody else to set at his side ... only we do complain that in this high order four admirals find a place. Are we then so rich in admiralty, so poor in literature? The same is still truer when we come to the inferior orders, which are still fairly high, such as the Commandership of the Bath. That ancient order is almost entirely recruited from amongst soldiers, sailors, politicians, and civil servants; it does not hold the name of a single novelist. No novelist is a Privy Councillor, though the position is honorific and demands no special knowledge. On the Privy Council you find labour members of Parliament, barristers, coal owners, sellers of chemicals and other commodities, but no novelists. In all the other orders it is the same thing; for novelists there are neither commanderships of the Bath, nor of the Victorian Order, nor of St Michael and St George, no honours great or minor; no man has ever in England been offered a peerage because he wrote novels; and yet he has been offered a peerage because he sold beer. George Meredith was not offered a peerage, even though some think that his name will live when those of captains and kings have melted into dust. Our little band of recognised men, such as Sir James Barrie, Sir Anthony Hope Hawkins, Sir Rider Haggard, Sir Arthur Conan Doyle, small is the toll they have taken of public recognition; perhaps they should not expect it; perhaps they have been recognised only because of certain political activities; but must we really believe that so many lawyers and so few writers are worthy of an accolade? Is the novelist worthless until he is dead?

This picture may seem too black, but it is that of Great Britain, where contempt for literature has risen to a peculiar degree. Make an imaginative effort; see yourself in the drawing-room of some social leader, where a 'crush' of celebrities is taking place. A flunkey at the head of the stairs announces the guests. He announces: 'Lord Curzon! ... Mr Joseph Conrad! ... The Bishop of London!' Who caused a swirl in the 'gilded throng?' The cleric? The politician? Or the novelist? Be honest in your reply, and you will know who, at that hypothetical reception, created a stir. The stir, according to place or period, greeted the politician or the bishop, and only in purely literary circles would Mr Conrad have been preferred.... For the worship of crowds goes to power rather than to distinction, to the recognised functionary of the State, to him whose power can give power, to all the evanescent things, and seldom to those stockish things, the milestones on the road to eternity. The attitude of the crowd is the attitude of the State, for the State is only the crowd, and often just the mob; it is the chamberlain of ochlocracy, the leader who follows. In all times, the State has shown its indifference, its contempt, for the arts, and particularly for literature. Now and then a prince, such as Louis of Bavaria, Philip of Spain, Lorenzo the Magnificent, has given to literature more than respect. He has given love, but that only because he was a man before a prince. The prince must prefer the lawyer, the politician, the general, and indeed, of late years what prince was found to patron George Meredith or Henry James?

The attitude of the State to the novelist defines itself most clearly when a royal commission is appointed. In England, royal commissions are ad hoc bodies appointed by the government from among men of political influence and special knowledge, to investigate a special question.

As a rule they are well composed. For instance, a royal commission on water supply would probably comprise two or three members of Parliament of some standing, the President of the Institute of Civil Engineers, a professor of sanitation, a canal expert, one or two trade unionists, one or two manufacturers, and a representative of the Home Office or the Board of Trade. Any man of position who has shown interest in public affairs may be asked to sit on a royal commission ... provided he is not a novelist. Only one novelist has attained so giddy a height: Sir Rider Haggard; how it happened is not known: it must have been a mistake. We are not weighty enough, serious enough to be called on, even if our novels are so weighty and so serious that hardly anybody can read them. We are a gay tribe of Ariels, too light to discuss even our own trade. For royal commissions concern themselves with our trade, with copyright law, with the restrictions of the paper supply. You might think that, for instance, paper supply concerned us, for we use cruel quantities, yet no recognised author sat on the commission; a publisher was the nearest approach. Apparently there were two great consumers of paper, authors and grocers, but alone the grocers were consulted. What is the matter with us? Is our crime that we put down in indecent ink what we think and feel, while other people think and feel the same, but prudently keep it down? Possibly our crimes are our imagination and our tendency to carry this imagination into action. Bismarck said that a State conducted on the lines of the Sermon on the Mount would not last twenty-four hours; perhaps it is thought that a State in the conduct of which a novelist had a share would immediately resolve itself into a problem play. Something like that, though in fact it is unlikely that Ariel come to judgment would be much more fanciful in his decrees than the historic Solomon.

All this because we lack solidity ... and yet the public calls us commercial, self-advertisers, money-grubbers. It is thought base that we should want three meals a day, though nobody suggests that we can hope to find manna in the street, or drink in our parks from the fountain Hippocrene. We are told that we make our contracts too keenly, that we are grasping, that we are not straight ... and yet we are told that we are not business men. What are we to do? Shall we form a trade union and establish a piece rate? Shall we sell our novels by the yard? May we not be as commercial and respected as the doctor who heals with words and the lawyer who strangles with tape? Now and then the defences of society and state are breached, and a novelist enters Parliament. Mr Hilaire Belloc, Mr A. E. W. Mason, followed Disraeli into the House of Commons, but it is very extraordinary. No one knows how these gentlemen managed to convince the electors that with their eye 'in fine frenzy rolling' they would not scandalise their party by voting against it. (Those writing chaps, you know, they aren't safe!)

It must be said that in Parliament the novelists did not have a very good time; they were lucky in having been preferred to a landowner or a pawnbroker, but once in they had not the slightest chance of being preferred to those estimable members of society. It was not a question of straight votes; it never came to that, for Mr Belloc soon disagreed with both sides and became a party of one, while Mr A. E. W. Mason as a rushlight flickered his little flicker and went out. It is as well; they would never have been taken seriously. It is almost a tradition that they should not be taken seriously, and it is on record in most of the worldly memoirs of the nineteenth century that the two main objections to Disraeli were his waistcoats and his authorship of Contarini Fleming. Nero liked to see people burnt alive; Disraeli wrote novels. Weaknesses are found in all great men.

There seems in this to lie error as well as scandal; when a new organisation is created, say for the control of lamp oil, obviously a novelist should not be made its chairman, but why should a blotting paper merchant be preferred? Indeed, one might side with Mr Zangwill, who demands representation for authors in the Cabinet itself, on the plea that they would introduce the emotion which is necessary if the Cabinet is to manage impulsive mankind. As he finely says, we are professors of human nature; if only some University would give us a title and some initials to follow our name, say P.H.N., people might believe that we knew something of it. But the attitude of the State in these matters is steadfast enough. It recognises us as servants rather than as citizens; if in our later years we come upon hard times, we can be given, through the Civil List, pensions which rescue us from the indignities of the poorhouse, but no more. Mostly these pensions benefit our heirs, but the offering is so small that it shocks; it is like tipping an archbishop. Thus Mr W. B. Yeats enjoys a pension of £150, Mr Joseph Conrad, of £100. Why give us pensions at all if they must be alms? One cannot be dignified on £100 a year; one can be dignified on £5000 a year, because the world soon forgets that you ride a gift horse if that horse is a fine, fat beast. The evidence is to be found in the retiring pensions of our late Lord Chancellors, who receive £5000 a year, of our Judges, £1000 to £3750, in the allowances made to impoverished politicians, which attain £2000. Out of a total of £320,000 met by our civil list, literature, painting, science, research, divide every year £1200. Nor do the immediate rewards show greater equality. Lord Roberts was voted £100,000 for his services in South Africa; Mr Thomas Hardy has not yet been voted anything for The Dynasts.

The shame of literature is carried on even into following generations. The present Lord Nelson, who is not a poor man, for he owns 7000 acres of land, is still drawing a pension of £5000 a year, earned by his august ancestor, but the daughter of Leigh Hunt must be content with £50. We are unknown. We are nobody. Rouget de l'Isle, author of La Marseillaise, gave wings to the revolutionary chariot, but tiny, bilious, tyrannic Robespierre rode in it, and rides in it to-day through the pages of history, while men go to their death singing the words of Rouget de l'Isle and know him not.

Even in our own profession of authorship the novelist is an object of disdain. We are less than the economists, the historians, the political writers: we amuse while they teach; they bore, and as they bore it is assumed that they educate, dullness always having been the sorry companion of education. Evidence is easily found; there exists a useful, short encyclopædia called Books That Count. It contains the names of about 4000 authors, out of whom only sixty-three are novelists. Divines whose sermons do not fetch a penny at the second-hand bookseller's, promoters of economic theories long disproved, partisan historians, mendacious travellers ... they crowd out of the 'books that count' the pale sixty-three novelists, all that is left of the large assembly that gave us Tom Jones and The Way of All Flesh. This attitude we observe in most reference books. We observe it, for instance, in the well-known Who's Who Year Book, which, amazing as it seems, contains no list of authors. The book contains a list of professors, including those of dental surgery, a list of past Presidents of the Oxford Union, a list of owners of Derby winners, but not a list of authors. The editors of this popular reference book know what the public wants; apparently the public wants to know that Mr Arthur H. King is General Manager of the Commercial Bank of London Ltd. ... but the public does not want to know that Mr Anatole France is a great man. The only evidence of notice is a list of our pseudonyms. It matters that Mr Richard Le Gallienne should write under the name of 'Logroller,' for that is odd. Mr Le Gallienne, being an author, is a curiosity; it matters to nobody that he is a man.

II

What is the area of a novelist's reputation? How far do the ripples extend when he casts a novel into the whirlpool of life? It is difficult to say, but few novelists were ever so well known to the people as were in their time such minor figures as Bradlaugh and Dr Grace, nor is there a novelist to-day whose fame can vie with that of, say, Mr Roosevelt. It is strange to think that Dickens himself could not in his own day create as much stir as, say, Lord Salisbury. He lacked political flavour; he was merely one of the latter day prophets who lack the unique advertisement of being stoned. It will be said that such an instance is taken from the masses of the world, most of whom do not read novels, while all are affected by the politician, but in those circles that support literature the same phenomenon appears; the novel may be known; the novelist is not. The novel is not respected and, indeed, one often hears a woman, at a big lending library, ask for 'three of the latest novels.' New novels! Why not new potatoes? She takes the books away calmly, without looking at the titles or the names. She is quite satisfied; sometimes she does not care much whether or not she has read those novels before, for she does not remember them. They go in at one ear and come out at the other presumably, as a judge said, because there is nothing to stop them.

It is undeniable that the great mass of readers forget either names or titles; many forget both. Some of the more educated remember the author and ask their library for 'something by E. M. Dell,' because she writes such sweet, pretty books, a definition where slander subtly blends with veracity. But, in most cases, nothing remains of either author or title except a hazy impression; the reader is not quite sure whether the book she liked so much is Fraternity or the Corsican Brothers. She will know that it had something to do with family, and that the author's name began with 'G' ... unless it was 'S'. It cannot be otherwise, so long as novels are read in the way they are read, that is to say, if they are taken as drugs. Generally, novels are read to dull the mind, and many succeed, ruining the chances of those whose intent is not morphean, which fulfil the true function of art, viz., to inflame. The object of a novel is not to send the reader to sleep, not to make him oblivious of time on a railway journey; it is meant to show character, to stimulate observation, to make life vivid, and as life is most vivid when it is most unpleasant, the novel that is worth reading is naturally set aside. For such novels stir the brain too much to let it go to sleep. Those novels are judged in the same way as the baser kind, and that is, perhaps, why the novel itself stands so low. It does stand low, at least in England, for it is almost impossible to sell it. Inquiries made of publishers show that they expect to sell to the circulating libraries seventy to seventy-five per cent. of the copies printed. To sell to a circulating library is not selling; it is lending at one remove; it means that a single copy bought by a library is read by anything between twenty and a hundred people. Sometimes it is read by more, for a copy bought by Mudie's is sold off when the subscribers no longer ask for it. It goes to a town of the size of, say Winchester. Discarded after a year or so by the subscribers it may be sold off for a penny or twopence, with one thrown into the dozen for luck, and arrive with its cover hanging on in a way that is a testimonial to the binder, with its pages marked with thumbs, stained with tears, or, as the case may be, with soup, at some small stationer's shop in a little market town, to go out on hire at a penny a week, until it no longer holds together, and goes to its eternal rest in the pulping machine. On the way, nobody has bought it except to let it out, as the padrone sends out the pretty Italian boys with an organ and a monkey. The public have not bought the book to read and to love. The twenty-five or thirty per cent. actually sold have been disposed of as birthday or Christmas presents, because one has to give something, and because one makes more effect with a well-bound book costing six shillings than with six shillings' worth of chocolates. Literature has been given its royalty on the bread of shame. Yet, impossible as the novel finds it to tear its shilling from the public, the theatre easily wheedles it into paying a guinea or more for two stalls. It seems strange that two people will pay a guinea to see Three Weeks on the boards, yet would never dream of giving four and sixpence for Miss Elinor Glyn's book. That is because theatre seats must be paid for, while books can be borrowed. It goes so far that novelists are continually asked 'where one can get their books,' meaning 'where they can be borrowed'; often they are asked to lend a copy, while no one begs a ride from a cabman.

In England, the public of the novel is almost exclusively feminine. Few men read novels, and a great many nothing at all except the newspaper. They say that they are too busy, which is absurd when one reflects how busy is the average woman. The truth is that they are slack and ignorant. They have some historic reason to despise the novel, for it is quite true that in the nineteenth century, with a few exceptions, such as Thackeray, Jane Austen, Charlotte Brontë, Nathaniel Hawthorne, Dickens, Scott, George Eliot, the three volume novel was trash. It dealt, generally, with some rhetorical Polish hero, a high-born English maiden, cruel parents, and Italian skies. Right up to 1885 that sort of thing used to arrive every morning outside Mudie's in a truck, but if it still arrives at Mudie's in a truck it should not be forgotten that other novels arrive. That is what the men do not know. If they read at all you will find them solemnly taking in The Reminiscences of Mr Justice X. Y. Z. or Shooting Gazelle in Bulbulland, Political Economics, or Economic Politics, (it means much the same either way up). All that sort of thing, that frozen, dried-up, elderly waggishness, that shallow pomp, is mentally murderous. Sometimes men do read novels, mostly detective stories, sporting or very sentimental tales. When observed, they apologise and say something about resting the brain. That means that they do not respect the books they read, which is base; it is like keeping low company, where one can yawn and put one's boots on the sofa. Now, no company is low unless you think it is. As soon as you realise that and stay, you yourself grow naturalised to it. Likewise, if you read a book without fellowship and respect for its author, you are outraging it. But mankind is stupid, and it would not matter very much that a few men should read novels in that shamefaced and patronising way if they were not so open about it. If they do not apologise, they boast that they never read a novel; they imply superiority. Their feminine equivalent is the serious-minded girl, who improves her mind with a book like Vicious Viscounts of Venice; if she reads novels at all she holds that like good wine they improve with keeping, and must be at least fifty years old. By that time the frivolous author may have redeemed his sins.

It is because of all these people, the people who borrow and do not cherish, the people who skim, the people who indulge and cringe, and the people who do not indulge at all, that we have come to a corruption of literary taste, where the idea is abashed before the easy emotion, where religiosity expels religion, and the love passion turns to heroics or to maundering, that the success of the second-rate, of Mrs Barclay, of Miss Gene Stratton Porter, of Mr Hall Caine, has come about. It is a killing atmosphere. It is almost incomprehensible, for when the talk is of a political proposal, say, of land settlement in South Africa, or of a new type of oil engine, hardly a man will say: 'I am not interested.' He would be ashamed to say that. It would brand him as a retrograde person. Sometimes he will say: 'I do not like music,' but he will avoid that if he can, for music is an evidence of culture; he will very seldom confess that he does not care for pictures; he will confess without any hesitation that he does not care for any kind of book. He will be rather proud to think that he prefers a horse or a golf-stick. It will seldom occur to him that this literature of which some people talk so much can hold anything for him. It will not even occur to him to try, for literature is judged at Jedburgh. It hardly ever occurs to any one that literature has its technique, that introductions to it are necessary; a man will think it worth while to join a class if he wants to acquire scientific knowledge, but seldom that anything in the novel justifies his taking preliminary steps. It is not that literature repels him by its occasional aridity; it is not that he has stumbled upon classics, which, as Mr Arnold Bennett delightfully says, 'are not light women who turn to all men, but gracious ladies whom one must long woo.' Men do not think the lady worth wooing. This brings us back to an early conclusion in this chapter; novelists are not useful; we are pleasant, therefore despicable. Our novels do not instruct; all they can do is to delight or inflame. We can give a man a heart, but we cannot raise his bank interest. So our novels are not worthy of his respect because they do not come clad in the staid and reassuring gray of the text-book; they are not dull enough to gain the respect of men who can appreciate only the books that bore them, who shrink away from the women who charm them and turn to those who scrag their hair off their forehead, and bring their noses, possibly with a cloth, to a disarming state of brilliancy.

Sometimes, when the novelist thinks of all these things, he is overcome by a desperate mood, decides to give up literature and grow respectable. He thinks of becoming a grocer, or an attorney, and sometimes he wants to be the owner of a popular magazine, where he will exercise, not the disreputable function of writing, but the estimable one of casting pleasant balance sheets. Then the mood passes, and he is driven back to Flaubert's view that it is a dog's life, but the only one. He decides to live down the extraordinary trash that novelists produce. Incredible as truth may be, fiction is stranger still, and there is no limit to the intoxications of the popular novelist. Consider, indeed, the following account of six novels, taken from the reviews in the literary supplement of the Times, of 27th July, 1916. In the first, Seventeen, Mr Booth Tarkington depicts characters of an age indicated by the title, apparently concerned with life as understood at seventeen, who conduct baby talk with dogs. In the second, Blow the Man Down, by Mr Holman Day, an American financier causes his ship to run ashore, while the captain is amorously pursued by the daughter of the villainous financier, and cuts his way out through the bottom of a schooner. The Plunderers, by Mr Edwin Lefevre, is concerned with robbers in New York, whose intentions are philanthropic; we observe also Wingate's Wife, by Miss Violet Tweedale, where the heroine suffers 'an agony of apprehension,' and sees a man murdered; but all is well, as the victim happens to be the husband whom she had deserted twenty years before. There is also The Woman Who Lived Again, by Mr Lindsey Russell, where a cabinet, in office when the war breaks out, concerns itself with German spies and an ancient Eurasian, who with Eastern secrets revives a dead girl and sends her back to England to confound the spies. There is also Because It Was Written, by Princess Radziwill, where Russian and Belgian horrors are framed in between a prologue and epilogue entirely devoted to archangels. There is nothing extraordinary in these novels; they merely happen to be reviewed on the same day. The collection compares perfectly with another, in the Daily News of the 19th September, 1916, where are reviewed a novel by Miss C. M. Matheson, one by Mr Ranger Gull, and one by 'Richard Dehan.' They are the usual sort of thing. The first is characterised by Mr Garnett as 'a hash of trite images and sentimental meanderings.' Miss Matheson goes so far as to introduce a shadowy, gleaming figure, which, with hand high upraised over the characters' heads, describes the Sign of the Cross. Mr Ranger Gull introduces as a manservant one of the most celebrated burglars of the day, a peer poisoned with carbon disulphide, wireless apparatus, and the lost heir to a peerage. As for 'Richard Dehan,' it is enough to quote one of her character's remarks: 'I had drained my cup of shame to the dregs.'

This sort of thing is produced in great abundance, and has helped to bring the novel down. Unreality, extravagance, stage tears, offensive piety, ridiculous abductions and machinery, because of those we have 'lost face,' like outraged Chinamen. No wonder that people of common intelligence, who find at their friend's house drivel such as this, should look upon the novel as unworthy. It is natural, though it is unjust. The novel is a commodity, and if it seeks a wide public it must make for a low one: the speed of a fleet is that of its slowest ship; the sale of a novel is the capacity of the basest mind. Only it might be remembered that all histories are not accurate, all biographies not truthful, all economic text-books not readable. Likewise, it should be remembered, and we need quote only Mr Conrad, that novels are not defined by the worst of their kind.... It is men's business to find out the best books; they search for the best wives, why not for the best novels? There are novels that one can love all one's life, and this cannot be said of every woman.

There are to-day in England about twenty men and women who write novels of a certain quality, and about as many who fail, but whose appeal is to the most intelligent. These people are trying to picture man, to describe their period, to pluck a feather from the wing of the fleeting time. They do not write about radium murders, or heroines clad in orchids and tiger skins. They strive to seize a little of the raw life in which they live. The claim is simple; even though we may produce two thousand novels a year which act upon the brain in the evening as cigarettes do after lunch, we do put forth a small number of novels which are the mirror of the day. Very few are good novels, and perhaps not one will live, but many a novel concerned with labour problems, money, freedom in love, will have danced its little dance to some purpose, will have created unrest, always better than stagnation, will have aroused controversy, anger, impelled some people, if not to change their life, at least to tolerate that others should do so. The New Machiavelli, Lord Jim, The White Peacock, The Rise of Silas Lapham, Ethan Frome, none of those are supreme books, but every one of them is a hand grenade flung at the bourgeoisie; we do not want to kill it, but we do want to wake it up.

It is the bourgeoisie's business to find out the novels that will wake it up; it should take as much pains to do this as to find out the best cigar. The bourgeoisie has congestion of the brain; the works of scholars will stupefy it still more; only in the novelists of the day, who are rough, unpleasant, rebellious, restless, will they find a remedy.

Whether the reading public can discern that undying flame in the choking smoke of books written for money and not for love, is another question. Every year more novels are published; but when one considers the novelists of the past, Thackeray's continual flow of sugary claptrap, the incapacity of Dickens to conceive beauty, the almost unrelieved, stagey solemnity of Walter Scott, the novelist of to-day is inclined to thank God that he is not as other men. Those old writers trod our paths for us, but they walked blindfold; let us recognise their splendid qualities, their feeling for atmosphere, their knowledge of men, but we find more that is honest and hopeful in a single page of Tono Bungay than in all the great Victorians put together. Yes, we are arrogant; why not? Why should it be natural to us to see our faults and not our talents? We are held in contempt, but such was the fate of every prophet; they make us into mummers and we learn mummery, but Balzac and Turgenev rise from their own dust. We are not safe people, or quiet people; not tame rabbits in a hutch, nor even romantic rogues: most of us are no more romantic than jockeys.

It is, perhaps, because we are not safe (and are we any less safe than company promoters?) that we are disliked. We are disliked, as Stendhal says, because all differences create hatred; because by showing it its face in the glass we tend to disrupt society, to exhibit to its shocked eyes what is inane in its political constitution, barbarous in its moral code. We are queer people, nasty people, but we are neither nastier nor queerer than our fellows. We are merely more shameless and exhibit what they hide. We have got outside, and we hate being outside; we should so much like to enlist under the modern standard, the silk hat, and yet we are arrogant. Doctors, judges, bishops, merchants, think little of us; we regret it and rejoice in it. We are unhappy and exalted adventurers in the frozen fields of human thought. We are the people who make the 'footprints on the sands of time.' Later on, the bourgeoisie will tread in them.

Who is the Man?

I

And so from hour to hour we ripe and ripe, and then from hour to hour we rot and rot. A gloomy saying, but one which applies to men as well as to empires, and to none, perhaps, more than to those men who stand in the vanguard of literature. Of very few writers, save those who were so fortunate as to be carried away by death in the plenitude of their powers (unless, like Mr Thomas Hardy, they drew back from the battle of letters) can it be said that the works of their later years were equal to those of their maturity. The great man has his heir in the world, one who impatiently waits for his shoes and is assured that he will fill them. It is well so, for shoes must be filled, and it is good to know the claimants.

Who are these men? Is it possible already to designate them? To mark out the Hardy or the Meredith of to-morrow? The Bennett, the Wells, or the Galsworthy? It is difficult. I shall not be surprised if some quarrel with these names, cavil at the selection and challenge a greatness which they look upon as transient. Those critics may be right. I do not, in this article, attempt a valuation of those whom I will call the literary novelists, that is to say, the men who have 'somehow,' and owing to hardly ascertained causes, won their way into the front rank of modern English letters. It may be urged that these are not our big men, and that the brazen blaring of popular trumpets has drowned the blithe piping of tenderer songsters. But, if we view facts sanely, we must all agree that there are in England five men, of whom one is a foreigner, who hold without challenge the premier position among novelists: Mr Arnold Bennett, Mr Joseph Conrad, Mr John Galsworthy, Mr Thomas Hardy, and Mr H. G. Wells. Theirs is a special position: there is not one of them, probably, whose sales would create envy in the bosom of Mr Harold Bell Wright or of Mrs Barclay; nor are they of the super-hyper class whose works are issued in wisely limited editions and printed in over-beautiful type. They are, in a very rough way, the men of their time and, a very little, the men of all time. Whatever be their greatness or their littleness, they are the men who will, for the University Extension Lecturer of 1950, represent the English novel in a given period; they are not the most literary of their contemporaries; they have not more ideas than some of their contemporaries, and all of them have their faults, their mannerisms, and their lapses, but yet, in a rough and general way, these five men combine more ideas with more style than any who are beyond their group. 'Somehow' they stand at the head, and I make no attempt to criticise them, to classify them: I have even named them in alphabetical order. Now not one of these men is under forty; one is over seventy; one approaches sixty. They must be replaced. Not yet, of course, though some of the young begin, a little rashly, to cast stones at those mature glories. But still, some time, faced as we are with a horde of novelists, not less in these islands than fifteen hundred, we must ask ourselves: Who are the young men who rear their heads above the common rank? Which ones among them are likely to inherit the purple?

II

In such an examination we must not ask for achievement, for by young men is meant those who have not passed, or have but lately passed, thirty. That they should show promise at all is remarkable enough, and distinguishes them from their forbears: while Mr Bennett, Mr Galsworthy, and Mr Conrad published no novel at all before they were thirty, and Mr Wells not much more than a fantastic romance, the young men of to-day tell a different tale. Mr J. D. Beresford, Mr Gilbert Cannan, Mr E. M. Forster, Mr D. H. Lawrence, Mr Compton Mackenzie, Mr Oliver Onions, Mr Frank Swinnerton, are a brilliant little stable, and have mostly tried their paces many years earlier; theirs have been the novels of the twenty-eight-year-old, in one case, at least, that of the twenty-six-year-old. They have affirmed themselves earlier than did their seniors and yet quite definitely.

The short list defies challenge, even though some may wish to include an obscurer favourite, some other young intellectual novelist or a more specialised man, such as Mr Algernon Blackwood, Mr Frederick Niven, or Mr James Stephens, or a recent discovery, such as Mr Alec Waugh, Mr J. W. N. Sullivan, Mr Stephen McKenna, or Mr James Joyce; still the classification is a very general one; it is almost undeniable that those are the men among whom will be recruited the leaders of to-morrow. Indeed I have neglected some aspirants, relegated them into a class which will, in a few years give us the inheritors of certain men of high literary quality who, owing to accident to style or to choice of subject, have not laid hands upon literary crowns. But that is inevitable. The seven men selected are those who show promise.

By promise is meant a suggestion that the young man will become a big man, that is to say that, in ten years or so, he will be the vehicle of the modern idea through the style of the time; he may not be very popular, but he will not be unpopular; he will be quoted, criticised, discussed; briefly, he will matter. Now I do not suggest that the seven men named will inevitably become big men. There is not room for seven big novelists, but it is among them that, in all likelihood, the two or three leaders will be found. And then there is the dark horse, still, perhaps, in some university, in America or in a colony, perhaps In a factory or a shop, who may sally forth, swift as a comet, and destroy our estimate; I have at least one such dark horse in my mind. But in a valuation we must reckon on the known, and it is submitted that we know nothing beyond this list.

The manner in which these men will express themselves cannot be determined absolutely. The literary tradition is changing, and a new one is being made. If the future is to give us a Balzac or a Fielding he will not write like a Balzac or a Fielding: he will use a new style. That is why there is very little hope for those who competently follow the tradition of the past. If a Madame Bovary were to be written to-day by a man of thirty it would not be a good book; it would be a piece of literary archæology. If the seven young men become the men of to-morrow, it will be because they break away from the old traditions, the tradition of aloofness and the tradition of comment. They do not rigidly stand outside the canvas, as did Flaubert and de Maupassant; nor do they obviously intervene as did Thackeray. If they look back at all it is to Dostoievsky and Stendhal, that is to say, they stand midway between the expression of life and the expression of themselves; indeed, they try to express both, to achieve art by 'criticising life'; they attempt to take nature into partnership. Only they do this to a greater or lesser extent; some do little more than exploit themselves, show the world in relation to their own autobiography; others hold up the mirror to life and interpose between picture and object the veil of their prejudice; and one of them is almost a commentator, for his prejudice is so strong as to become a protagonist in his drama. All this is to be expected, for one cannot expect a little group of seven which enjoys the high honour of having been selected from among fifteen hundred, to be made up of identical entities. Indeed, all must be contrasting persons: if two of them were alike, one would be worthless. And so each one has his devil to exorcise and his guardian-angel to watch over him. They must, each one of them, beware of exploiting themselves overmuch of becoming dull as they exhaust their own history of being cold if they draw too thin a strand of temperament across the object which they illumine. But these dangers are only the accidents of a dangerous trade, where a man hazards his soul and may see it grow sick. If we wish to measure these dangers, we must then analyse the men one by one, and it will serve us best to divide them into three groups: self-exploiters, mirror-bearers, and commentators. These are not exact divisions; they overlap on one another; one man denies by one book what he affirms by a second. But, in a very rough way these divisions will serve: hesitations and contradictions indicate, indeed better than achievement, the tempestuous course of promising youth.

III

Though, broadly speaking, the seven young men are profoundly interested in themselves, there are four that attach especial importance to the life which has made them what they are. Messrs Cannan, Walpole, Beresford, and Lawrence, capable though they be of standing outside themselves, are, without much doubt, happier when they stand inside. I do not know in extreme detail where they were born or what they suffered, but it demands no great sagacity to reconstruct, for instance, Mr Walpole as a man who went to Cambridge, taught in a school, and later wrote books; likewise Mr Beresford, as one who struggled up against poverty and physical infirmity into a place in the sunshine of letters; Mr Cannan is still more emphatically interested in the reactions of his own harsh and sensitive temperament, while Mr Lawrence, a little more puzzling, is very much the lover of life, telling us tales of his mistress. This is not, perhaps, because they take these facts that lie nearest to their hand as the argument of their play. Each one of them has shown by some excursion that he was capable of jerking the earth off its axis, the axis being, with him as with all of us, his own personality. Thus Mr Cannan, in Peter Homunculus, presents in Meredithian wise, a picture of the development of a very young man, a rather romantic though metallically brilliant young man predestined by nature to have a bad, but very exciting time: that is Mr Cannan. More clearly still, in Little Brother, he takes himself up again, himself wondering in Cambridge 'what it's all for,' as Mr Wells would say, wondering still more, and still more vainly, when he enters London's cultured circles, from which he escapes through an obscure byway of Leicester Square. And then again, in Round the Corner, it is, a very little, Mr Cannan in Manchester, incredulously examining, and through Serge commenting upon the world. Were it not for Devious Ways one would be inclined to think that Mr Cannan had nothing to say except about himself, and, indeed, it is disquieting to think that the book which saves him from such a conclusion is inferior to his subjective work. Still, it is not altogether a bad book; it is not the sort of book with which Mr Cannan will bid for fame, but it represents the streak of detachment which is essential if this author is to show himself able to stand outside his own canvas; moreover, in Round the Corner, Mr Cannan was less limited by himself than he was in his previous books. The praise that has been showered on this novel was perfervid and indiscriminate; it was not sufficiently taken into account that the book was congested, that the selection of details was not unerring, and that the importation of such a character as Serge laid the author open to the imputation of having recently read Sanin; but, all this being said, it is certain that Round the Corner, with its accurate characterisation, its atmospheric sense and its diversity, marked a definite stage in the evolution of Mr Cannan. Though refusing to accept it as work of the first rank, I agree that it is an evidence of Mr Cannan's ability to write work of the first rank: he may never write it, but this book is his qualification for entering the race. His later novels, Young Earnest and Mendel, have done him no good; they are too closely related to his own life; his private emotions are also too active in his pacifist skit, Windmills, which is inferior to The Tale of a Tub. Other novels, too, such as Three Pretty Men and The Stucco House, exhibit painful superiority over the ordinary person; lacking humour, it seems that Mr Cannan has taken himself too seriously, one might almost say, too dramatically; those sufferings, misunderstandings, isolations, and struggles of his youth have been to him too vivid and too significant. For a long time his picture fogged his vision; he could not see himself for himself. But he may come to view more sanely the epic of his own life and more wholly the epic of the life of others. If he will consent to be less the actor and more the spectator, he will probably succeed in becoming the playwright.

Mr Walpole does not, so definitely as Mr Cannan, view the world in terms of his own life, his personality is otherwise tinged: he is less angry, less chafed, and it may be that because he is of the softer Southern breed, he has no share in the dour aggressiveness of Mr Cannan's North country. And there is a variation in the self that Mr Walpole paints: it is not what he is, or even what he thinks he is, but what he would like to be. In his chief work, by which is meant the most artistic, Mr Perrin and Mr Traill, the writer shares with us much of the wistfulness he must have felt in his early manhood, but Mr Traill is not Mr Walpole; if he were, he would have recurred in other novels; he is the simple, delicate, and passionate young man (passionate, that is, in the modest English way), that Mr Walpole would like to be. This we know because Mr Walpole loves Traill and sees no weakness in him: now, one may love that which one despises, but that which one admires one must love. No lover can criticise his lady, if his lady she is to remain, and thus, in his incapacity to see aught save charm in his hero, Mr Walpole indicates the direction of his own desire. Yet, and strangely enough, in The Prelude to Adventure, there is a suggestion that Mr Walpole would gladly be Dune, haughty and sombre; in Fortitude, that he would be Peter Westcott, have his fine courage, his delicacy and his faith. He asks too much in wishing to be Proteus, but, in so doing, he puts forward a claim to talent, for he tells us his aspiration rather than his realisation. Indeed, if it were not that The Prelude to Adventure is so very much his life in Cambridge, Mr Perrin and Mr Traill his career in a little school, Fortitude his life under the influence of London's personality, he would not come into the class of those men who make copy of their past. And it is a feature of high redeeming value that in Maradick at Forty, he should have attempted to make copy of his future, for, again, here is aspiration. Mr Walpole needs to increase his detachment and widen the fields which he surveys. Schools and Cambridge: these are tales of little boys and their keepers; literary London: that is the grasshopper and its summer singing. He needs to develop, to embrace business and politics, the commonness of love, and the vital roughness of the world. He has tried to do this in The Dark Forest, but this is so close a pastiche of Russian novels that it cannot stand for Mr Walpole's emancipation.

IV

In Mr Beresford we discover a closer identity between the man and the mask, though he has written several books where he does not figure, The Hampdenshire Wonder, the tale of an incredible child, The

House in Demetrius Road, and Goslings, a fantastic commentary upon life. Mr Beresford is more at his ease when he tells his own tale. In three books, The Early History of Jacob Stahl, A Candidate for Truth, and The Invisible Event, Mr Beresford has exploited himself with some eloquence; he has the sense of selection, he is not crabbed, and he informs with fine passion those early years through which fleets a fine woman figure. In these books, as also in Housemates, Mr Beresford shows that he knows love, and isolation, and pain: those other young men with whom we are concerned feel these things, too, but hardly one so passionately. Mr Beresford's merit is that he is more ordinary, thus that he is less unreal than the passionate persons his rivals are or would be. Yet, if this were all, it might not be enough, for a tale may be told twice but not more often; if, in the first part of Goslings, Mr Beresford had not shown how closely and incisively he can picture the lower-middle class, analyse its ambitions, sympathise with its hopes, his would be a limited scope. I hope he will go further in this direction, extend his criticism of life through more of those people and more of their fates, while he himself remains outside. He must choose: Jacob Stahl, that is Mr Beresford, is a charming creature whom one would gladly know; but Jasper Thrale, expounding the world, is not Mr Beresford, for he is a prig. Mr Beresford may run on two lines: one for himself alone, and one for the world as he sees it.

Mr D. H. Lawrence's is not in the same class. Once only can he have been autobiographical; either in The White Peacock, or in Sons and Lovers, for he could evidently not have been, at the same time, the poetic son of a collier and a cultured member of the well-to-do classes in a farming community. Probably it is an open secret that Mr Lawrence is closer to the Nottingham collier than to the rustic who made hay while others played Bach. But it does not matter very much whether he be one or the other; it is not his physical self he puts into his books, but the adventures of his temperament. It is a curious temperament, a mixture of Northern brutality with wistful Northern melancholy. His characters, and this applies to George and Lettice in The White Peacock, to Sigmund, in The Trespasser, to Paul Morel, Mrs Morel, and Miriam, in Sons and Lovers, are always battling with adversity for the sake of their fine hopes, are held up by their pride, and divorced a little from commoner folk by the taste that takes them to Verlaine and Lulli. If it is Mr Lawrence to whom every flower of the hedge and every feather of the strutting cock cries colour and passionate life, if it is for him that the water-meadows are fragrant and the star-lit nights endless deep, it is not for him that the characters live, but for us: he takes his share, he leaves us ours; he inflames his characters, then allows them to act. Indeed, if no fault were to be found with him on mere literary score, Mr Lawrence would be more than a man of promise: he would have arrived. But his passion carries him away; he sees too much, shows too much, he analyses too fully, discovers too many elements. It may be urged that no artist can see or analyse too fully. But he can, if he discovers that which is not there. Mr Lawrence, having found gold in the dross of common men and women, is inclined to infer that there is too much gold in the vulgar. Being convinced of this, he becomes hectic; his people are as flames, feeding upon mortal bodies and burning them up. His peril is excessive sensation. He needs some better knowledge of affairs, more intercourse with the cruder rich, with the drab middle-class, so that his brilliant vision may by its dulling become tolerable to meaner eyes. He needs to discover those for whom music hath no charms, and yet are not base in attitude.

Mr Lawrence, who exploits his life not over much, affords us a necessary transition between those who are interested in little else and the second group, Mr Mackenzie, Mr Onions, and Mr Swinnerton, who have, with more or less success, tried to stand back as they write. Of these, Mr Compton Mackenzie is the most interesting because, in three volumes, he has made three new departures: The Passionate Elopement, a tale of powder and patches; Carnival, a romance of the meaner parts of London and of Charing Cross Road, and lastly Sinister Street, where he links up with those who exploit only their experiences. Evidently Mr Mackenzie believes that a good terrier never shakes a rat twice. Had Sinister Street been his first contribution to literature, Mr Mackenzie would have found his place indicated in the first group, but as he began by standing outside himself it must be assumed that he thought it a pity to let so much good copy go begging. He is a man difficult of assessment because of his diversity. He has many graces of style, and a capacity which may be dangerous of infusing charm into that which has no charm. He almost makes us forget that the heroine of Carnival is a vulgar little Cockney, by tempting us to believe that it might have been otherwise with her. There is a cheapness of sentiment about this Jenny, this Islington columbine, but we must not reproach Mr Mackenzie for loving his heroine over-much: too many of his rivals are not loving theirs enough. Indeed, his chief merit is that he finds the beautiful and the lovable more readily than the hideous. His figures can serve as reagents against the ugly heroine and the scamp hero who grew fashionable twenty years ago. His success, if it comes at all, will be due to his executive rather than to his artistic quality, for he often fails to sift his details. In Sinister Street, we endure a great congestion of word and interminable catalogues of facts and things. If he has a temperament at all, which I believe, it is stifled by the mantle in which he clothes it. It is not that Mr Mackenzie knows too much about his characters, for that is not possible, but he tells us too much. He does not give our imagination a chance to work. His romantic earnestness, as shown in Guy and Pauline, is unrelieved by humour and makes those details wearisome. Yet, his hat is in the ring. If he can prune his efflorescent periods and select among his details he may, by force of charm, attain much further than his fellows. He will have to include just those things and no others which can give us an illusion of the world.

V

In direct opposition to Mr Mackenzie, we find Mr Onions. While Mr Mackenzie gives us too much and allows us to give nothing, Mr Onions gives us hardly anything and expects us to write his novel for him as we read it. There are two strands in his work, one of them fantastic and critical, the other creative. Of the first class are the tales of Widdershins, and The Two Kisses, a skit on studios and boarding-houses. Even slightly more massive works, such as the love epic of advertisement, Good Boy Seldom, and the fierce revelation of disappointment which is in Little Devil Doubt do not quite come into the second class; they are not the stones on which Mr Onions is to build. They are a destructive criticism of modern life, and criticism, unless it is creative, is a thing of the day, however brilliant it may seem. Mr Oliver Onions can be judged only on his trilogy, In Accordance with the Evidence, The Debit Account, and The Story of Louie, for these are creative works, threaded and connected; they are an attempt and, on the whole, a very successful one, to take a section of life and to view it from different angles. If the attempt has not completely succeeded, it is perhaps because it was too much. It rests upon close characterisation, a sense of the iron logic of facts and upon atmospheric quality. There is not a young man, and for the matter of that an old one, more than Mr Onions, capable of anatomical psychology. There may be autobiography in some of Mr Onions's work, but there is in his trilogy no more than should colour any man's book.

Yet Mr Onions has his devil, and it takes the form of a rage against the world, of a hatred that seems to shed a bilious light over his puppets. His strong men are hard, almost brutal, inconsiderate, dominant only by dint of intellect, and arrogant in their dominance; his weak men are craven, lying, incapable of sweetness; even strong Louie is so haughty as almost to be rude. All this appears in the very style, so much so that, were it not for the cliché, I would quote Buffon. The sentences are tortured as if born in agony; the highly selected detail is reluctant, avaricious, as if Mr Onions hated giving the world anything. And yet, all this culminates in an impression of power: Mr Onions is the reticent man whose confidence, when earned, is priceless. He lays no pearls before us; he holds them in his half-extended hand for us to take if we can. Some tenderness; some belief that men can be gentle and women sweet; a little more hope and some pity, and Mr Onions will be judged more fairly.

Of Mr Swinnerton, who also stands outside his canvas, one is not so sure. He made, in The Casement, an elusive picture of the life of the well-to-do when confronted with the realities of life, but did not succeed emphatically enough in the more ponderous effort entitled The Happy Family. There he was too uniform, too mechanical, and rather too much bound by literary traditions. He was so bound also in his brilliant Nocturne, the tragedy of five creatures within a single night. But Mr Swinnerton has a point of view, an attitude toward life; I could not define it, but am conscious of its existence, and in a man of promise that is quite enough. For a man with an individual attitude will make it felt if he has the weapons of style with which to express it. Now Mr Swinnerton shows great dexterity in the use of words, felicity of phrase, a discrimination in the choice of details which will enable him to embody such ideas as he may later on conceive. He has only to fear that he may be mistaken as to the size of his ideas; like Mr Hugh de Selincourt, he may be too much inclined to take as the plot of a novel an idea and a story in themselves too slender. Under modern publishing conditions he may be compelled to spin out his work: as his tendency is to concentrate, he may find himself so much hampered as to lose the chief charm of his writing, viz., balance. He has shown charm in Nocturne, some power in The Happy Family; these two qualities need blending, so that Mr Swinnerton be no longer two men, but one.

Brief mention must be made of Mr Perceval Gibbon. Of his novels, one only, Souls in Bondage, showed remarkable promise, but his later work with the exception of a few short stories, was disappointing. In that book there was colour, atmosphere, characterisation and technique, but there was also passion. The passion was not maintained in later years. Other qualities were still there: he knows how to express the dusty glare or the dank warmth of the tropics, the languor, veiling fire, of its men and women, but the vision is a little exterior. Mr Gibbon needs to state his point of view, if he has one, to let us see more clearly how he himself stands in relation to the world. This does not apply to Mr de Selincourt, somewhat afflicted with moral superciliousness, whose point of view is one of aloof vigour. To a great charm of style he adds selectiveness; in A Daughter of the Morning, the characterisation is inwrought, just as in A Boy's Marriage it is passionate. And again there is Mr C. E. Montague, all bathed in the glamour of George Meredith and Mr Henry James. Of these Mr de Selincourt is by far the most interesting; he has elected to depict not the people who live ill, but those whom he conceives as living well, proud of their body, responsible to their instincts. In A Soldier of Life, notably, he makes almost credible the regeneration of the 'ordinary' man. Still, they are difficult to classify, these three; to reject their candidature may be too much, so fine are their qualities; and yet, to inscribe them upon the roll may be undue, for they have not the raw massiveness, the air that one wants to find in boys, about to be men; they are too particular, too much inclined to look away from the world and to concentrate on some microscopic section. To enlarge without loosening is no easy matter.

Lastly, and by himself, there is Mr E. M. Forster, who has been forgotten a little in a hurry, because he has not, since 1910, felt inclined to publish a novel; he is still one of the young men, while it is not at all certain that he is not 'the' young man. Autobiography has had its way with him, a little in A Room With a View, and very much more in that tale of schoolmasters, The Longest Journey; but it was Howard's End, that much criticised work, which achieved the distinction of being popular, though of high merit. This marks out Mr Forster and makes it likely that he can climb Parnassus if he chooses. In Howard's End Mr Forster surveyed the world in particular and also in general; he was together local and cosmic; he was conscious of the little agitations and artificialities of the cultured, of the upthrust of the untaught and of the complacent strength of those who rule. Over all, hung his own self as the wings of a roc darkening the countryside. It is because Mr Forster has seized a portion of the world and welded it with himself that the essence of him may persist and animate other worlds. His attitude is one of tolerance; he prays that we may not drift too far from the pride of body which is the pride of spirit. Mystic athleticism: that seems to be Mr Forster's message; as it is essential that the man of to-morrow should be a man of ideas as well as a man of perceptions, it is quite certain that, if Mr Forster chooses to return to the field, he will establish his claim.

One word as to women. The time has gone when we discriminated between the work of women and of men; to-day, 'Lucas Malet,' Miss May Sinclair, Mrs Sedgwick, Mrs Edith Wharton, Miss Violet Hunt, Miss Ethel Sidgwick, Mrs Belloc-Lowndes, and Mrs Dudeney, must take their chance in the rough and tumble of literary criticism, and the writer does not suggest a comparison between them and the leading men. For this there is a very good reason: the young women of to-day are promising work of an entirely new kind. They have less style than their precursors and more ideas: such women writers as Miss Amber Reeves,[3] Miss Viola Meynell, Miss Sheila Kaye-Smith,[4] Miss Tennyson Jesse, Miss Dorothy Richardson, Miss Katherine Gerould, Miss Bridget MacLagan have produced so far, very little; they can be indicated as candidates, but much more faintly than their masculine rivals. They write less, and less easily; they are younger at their trade, more erratic. It is enough to mention them, and to say that, so far as women are showing indications of approximating to men in literary quality, these are the women who are likely soon to bear the standards of their sex.

[3: See Special Chapter.]

[4: Ibid.]

To sum up, I suggest that the rough classification of the seven young men must not be taken as fixed. Some are more autobiographic than evocative; some are receptive rather than personally active, and yet others have not chosen between the two roads. Yet, taking them as a whole, with the reservation of possible dark horses, these are probably the men among whom will be found the two or three who will 'somehow,' in another ten years, lead English letters. It will be an indefinable 'somehow,' a compound of intellectual dominance and emotional sway. We shall not have a Bennett for a Bennett, nor a Wells for a Wells, but equivalents of power, and equivalents of significance, who will be intimately in tune with their time and better than any will express it.

Three Young Novelists

1. MR D. H. LAWRENCE

It is not a very long time ago since Professor Osler startled America and England by proclaiming that a man was too old at forty. This is not generally held, though, I suppose, most of us will accept that one is too old to begin at forty. But that is not the end: very soon, in literature at least, it may be too late to begin at thirty, if we are to take into account the achievements of the young men, of whom Mr D. H. Lawrence is one of the youngest. Mr Lawrence is certainly one of the young men, not a member of a school, for they have no formal school, and can have none if they are of any value, but a partner in their tendencies and an exponent of their outlook. He has all the unruliness of the small group that is rising up against the threatening State, its rules and its conventions, proclaiming the right of the individual to do much more than live—namely, to live splendidly.

It is this link makes Mr Lawrence so interesting; this fact that, like them, he is so very much of his time, so hot, controversial, uneasy; that, like them, he has the sudden fury of the bird that beats against the bars of its cage. But while the young men sneer at society, at the family, at every institution, Mr Lawrence tends to accept these things; he has no plan of reform, no magic wand with which to transmute the world into fairyland: he claims only as a right to develop his individuality, and to see others develop theirs, within a system which tortures him as another Cardinal La Balue.

This it is differentiates him from so many of his rivals. He has in his mind no organisations; he is mainly passionate aspiration and passionate protest. And that is not wonderful when we consider who he is. Surprising to think, this prominent young novelist is only thirty-four. Son of a Nottinghamshire coal-miner, a Board-school boy, his early career seems to have been undistinguished: a county council scholarship made of him a school teacher, imparting knowledge in the midst of old-fashioned chaos in a room containing several classes. Then another scholarship, two years at college, and Mr Lawrence went to Croydon to teach for less than £2 a week. Then the literary life, though I extract from his record the delightful fact that at college they gave him prizes for history and chemistry, but placed him very low in the English class. (This is rather embarrassing for those who believe in the public endowment of genius.)

I have said 'then the literary life,' but I was wrong, for already at twenty-one Mr Lawrence had begun The White Peacock, of which, year by year, and he confesses often during lectures, he was laying the foundations. Mr Lawrence did not, as do so many of us, enter the literary life at a given moment: literature grew in him and with him, was always with him, even in the worst years of his delicate health. If literature was not his passion, it was to his passion what the tongue is to speech: the essential medium of his expression.

Sometimes when reading one of his works, I wonder whether Mr Lawrence has not mistaken his medium, and whether it is not a painter he ought to have been, so significant is for him the slaty opalescence of the heron's wing and so rutilant the death of the sun. When he paints the countryside, sometimes in his simplicity he is almost Virgilian, but more often he is a Virgil somehow strayed into Capua and intoxicated with its wines. All through his novels runs this passionate streak, this vision of nature in relation to himself. But it is certainly in The White Peacock that this sensation attains its apogee. It is not a story which one can condense. Strictly, it is not a story at all. It presents to us a group of well-to-do people, cultured, and yet high in emotional tone.

Mr Lawrence himself, who figures in it, is effaced; Lettice, wayward and beautiful, is the fragrance of sex, but not more so than the honeysuckle in the hedges; George, muscles rippling under his skin, insensitive to cruelty, yet curiously moved by delicacy, is the brother of the bulls he herds; and all the others, the fine gentlemen, the laughing girls, farmers, school teachers, making hay, making music, making jokes, walking in the spangled meadows, and living, and wedding, and dying, all of them come to no resolution. Their lives have no beginning and no end. Mr Lawrence looks: Pippa passes. It is almost impossible to criticise The White Peacock, and the danger in an appreciation is that one should say too much good of it, for the book yields just the quality of illusion that a novel should give us, which does not of itself justify the critic in saying that it is a great book. For the novel, equally with the picture, can never reproduce life; it can only suggest it, and when it does suggest it, however peculiarly or partially, one is inclined to exaggerate the impression one has received and to refrain from considering whether it is a true impression. It is the vividness of Mr Lawrence's nature-vision carries us away; such phrases as these deceive us: 'The earth was red and warm, pricked with the dark, succulent green of bluebell sheaths, and embroidered with gray-green clusters of spears, and many white flowerets. High above, above the light tracery of hazel, the weird oaks tangled in the sunset. Below in the first shadows drooped hosts of little white flowers, so silent and sad, it seemed like a holy communion of pure wild things, numberless, frail and folded meekly in the evening light.' They deceive us because Mr Lawrence's realisation of man is less assured than his realisation of nature. I doubt the quality of his people's culture, the spontaneity of their attitude towards the fields in which they breathe; their spontaneity seems almost artificial.

That impression Mr Lawrence always gives; he sees the world through a magnifying-glass, and perhaps more so in Sons and Lovers than in The White Peacock. In that book he gives us unabashed autobiography—the story of his early youth, of his relation to his mother, a creature of fitful, delicate charm. Mrs Morel is very Northern; she has, with the harshness of her latitude, its fine courage and its ambition; Paul Morel, the hero, is Mr Lawrence himself, the little blue flower on the clinker heap. And those other folk about him, dark Miriam, slowly brooding over him; her rival, that conquering captive of sex; the brothers, the sisters, and the friends; this intense society is vital and yet undefinably exaggerated. Perhaps not so undefinably, for I am oppressed by unbelief when I find this grouping of agriculturists and colliers responding to the verse of Swinburne and Verlaine, to Italian, to Wagner, to Bach. I cannot believe in the spinet at the pit's mouth. And yet all this, Mr Lawrence tells us, is true! Well, it is true, but it is not general, and that is what impairs the value of Mr Lawrence's visions. Because a thing is, he believes that it is; when a thing is, it may only be accidental; it may be particular. Now one might discuss at length whether a novelist should concentrate on the general or on the particular, whether he should use the microscope or the aplanetic lense, and many champions will be found in the field. I will not attempt to decide whether he should wish, as Mr Wells, to figure all the world, or as Mr Bennett, to take a section; probably the ideal is the mean. But doubtless the novelist should select among the particular that which has an application to the general, and it may safely be said that, if Mr Lawrence errs at all, it is in selecting such particular as has not invariably a universal application.

Mr Lawrence lays himself open to this criticism in a work such as Sons and Lovers, because it has a conscious general scope, but in The Trespasser his conception is of a lesser compass. The book holds a more minute psychological intention. That Sigmund should leave his wife for another love and find himself driven to his death by an intolerable conflict between his desire, the love he bears his children, and the consciousness of his outlawry, should have made a great book. But this one of Mr Lawrence's novels fails because the author needs a wide sphere within which the particular can evolve; he is clamouring within the narrow limits of his incident; Sigmund appears small and weak; unredeemed by even a flash of heroism; his discontented wife, her self-righteous child hold their own views, and not enough those of the world which contains them. An amazing charge to make against a novelist, that his persons are too much persons! But persons must partly be types, or else they become monsters.

It would be very surprising if Mr Lawrence were not a poet in verse as well as in prose, if he did not sing when addressing his love:—

'Coiffing up your auburn hair In a Puritan fillet, a chaste white snare To catch and keep me with you there So far away.'

But a poet he is much more than a rebel, and that distinguishes him from the realists who have won fame by seeing the dunghill very well, and not at all the spreading chestnut-tree above. Though he select from the world, he is greedy for its beauty, so greedy that from all it has to give, flower, beast, woman, he begs more:—

'You, Helen, who see the stars As mistletoe berries burning in a black tree, You surely, seeing I am a bowl of kisses, Should put your mouth to mine and drink of me,'

'Helen, you let my kisses steam Wasteful into the night's black nostrils; drink Me up, I pray; oh, you who are Night's Bacchante, How can you from my bowl of kisses shrink!'

I cannot, having no faith in my power to judge poetry, proclaim Mr Lawrence to Parnassus, but I doubt whether such cries as these, where an urgent wistfulness mingles in tender neighbourhood with joy and pain together coupled, can remain unheard.

And so it seems strange to find in Mr Lawrence activities alien a little to such verses as these, to have to say that he is also an authoritative critic of German literature, and the author of a prose drama of colliery life. More gladly would I think of him always as remote from the stirrings of common men, forging and nursing his dreams. For dreams they are, and they will menace the realities of his future if he cannot 'breathe upon his star and detach its wings.' It is not only the dragon of autobiography that threatens him. It is true that so far he has written mainly of himself, of the world in intimate relation with himself, for that every writer must do a little; but he has followed his life so very closely, so often photographed his own emotions, that unless life holds for him many more adventures, and unless he can retain the power to give minor incident individual quality, he may find himself written out. For Mr Lawrence has not what is called ideas. He is stimulated by the eternal rather than by the fugitive; the fact of the day has little significance for him; thus, if he does not renew himself he may become monotonous, or he may cede to his more dangerous tendency to emphasise overmuch. He may develop his illusion of culture among the vulgar until it is incredible; he may be seduced by the love he bears nature and its throbbings into allowing his art to dominate him. Already his form is often turgid, amenable to no discipline, tends to lead him astray. He sees too much, feels significances greater than the actual; with arms that are too short, because only human, he strives to embrace the soul of man. This is exemplified in his last novel, The Rainbow, of which little need be said, partly because it has been suppressed, and mainly because it is a bad book. It is the story of several generations of people so excessive sexually as to seem repulsive. With dreadful monotony the women exhibit riotous desire, the men slow cruelty, ugly sensuality; they come together in the illusion of love and clasp hatred within their joined arms. As in Sons and Lovers, but with greater exaggeration, Mr Lawrence detects hate in love, which is not his invention, but he magnifies it into untruth. His intensity of feeling has run away with him, caused him to make particular people into monsters that mean as little to us, so sensually crude, so flimsily philosophical are they, as any Medusa, Medea, or Klytemnestra. The Rainbow, as also some of Mr Lawrence's verse, is the fruit of personal angers and hatreds; it was born in one of his bad periods from which he must soon rescue himself. If he cannot, then the early hopes he aroused cannot endure and he must sink into literary neurasthenia.

2. AMBER REEVES

'I don't agree with you at all.' As she spoke I felt that Miss Amber Reeves would have greeted as defiantly the converse of my proposition. She stood in a large garden on Campden Hill, where an at-home was proceeding, her effect heightened by Mr Ford Madox Hueffer's weary polish, and the burning twilight of Miss May Sinclair. Not far off Mr Wyndham Lewis was languid and Mr Gilbert Cannan eloquently silent. Miss Violet Hunt, rather mischievous, talked to Mr Edgar Jepson, who obviously lay in ambush, preparing to slay an idealist, presumably Sir Rabindrahath Tagore. I felt very mild near this young lady, so dark in the white frock of simplicity or artifice, with broad cheeks that recalled the rattlesnake, soft cheeks tinted rather like a tea rose, with long, dark eyes, wicked, aggressive, and yet laughing. I felt very old—well over thirty. For Miss Reeves had just come down from Newnham, and, indeed, that afternoon she was still coming down ... on a toboggan. When I met her the other day she said: 'Well, perhaps you are right.' It's queer how one changes!

She was about twenty-three, and that is not so long ago; she was still the child who has been 'brought up pious,' attended Sunday School and felt a peculiar property in God. Daughter of a New Zealand Cabinet Minister and of a mother so rich in energy that she turned to suffrage the scholarly Mr Pember Reeves, Miss Amber Reeves was a spoilt child. She was also the child of a principle, had been sent to Kensington High School to learn to be democratic and meet the butcher's daughter. She had been to Newnham too, taken up socialism, climbed a drain pipe and been occasionally sought in marriage. At ten she had written poems and plays, then fortunately gave up literature and, as a sponge flung into the river of life, took in people as they were, arrived at the maxim that things do not matter but only the people who do them. A last attempt to organise her took place in the London School of Economics, where she was to write a thesis; one sometimes suspects that she never got over it.

This is not quite just, for she is changed. Not hostile now, but understanding, interested in peculiarities as a magpie collecting spoons. Without much illusion, though; her novels are the work of a faintly cynical Mark Tapley.

She is driven to mimic the ordinary people whom she cannot help loving, who are not as herself, yet whom she forgives because they amuse her. She is still the rattlesnake of gold and rose, but (zoological originality) one thinks also of an Italian greyhound with folded paws, or a furred creature of the bush that lurks and watches with eyes mischievous rather than cruel.

On reading this over again I discover that she has got over the London School of Economics, though her first two books showed heavy the brand of Clare Market. Miss Amber Reeves started out to do good, but has fortunately repented. She has not written many novels, only three in five years, an enviable record, and they were good novels, with faults that are not those of Mrs Barclay or of Mr Hall Caine. Over every chapter the Blue Book hovered. Her first novel, The Reward of Virtue, exhibited the profound hopelessness of youth. For Evelyn Baker, daughter of a mother who was glad she was a girl because 'girls are so much easier,' was doomed to lead the stupid life. Plump, handsome, fond of pink, she lived in Notting Hill, went to dances, loved the artist and married the merchant, knew she did not love the merchant and went on living with him; she took to good works, grew tired of them, and gave birth to a girl child, thanking fate because 'girls are so much easier.' The story of Evelyn is so much the story of everybody that it seems difficult to believe it is the story of anybody. But it is. The Reward of Virtue is a remarkable piece of realism, and it is evidence of taste in a first novel to choose a stupid heroine, and not one who plays Vincent d'Indy and marries somebody called Hugo.

In that book Miss Amber Reeves indicated accomplishment, but this was rather slight; only in her second novel, A Lady and Her Husband, was she to develop her highest quality: the understanding of the ordinary man. (All young women novelists understand the artist, or nobody does; the man they seldom understand is the one who spends fifty years successfully paying bills.) The ordinary man is Mr Heyham, who runs tea shops and easily controls a handsome wife of forty-five, while he fails to control Fabian daughters and a painfully educated son. He runs his tea shops for profit, while Mrs Heyham comes to the unexpected view that he should run them for the good of his girls. There is a revolution in Hampstead when she discovers that Mr Heyham does not, for the girls are sweated; worse still, she sees that to pay them better will not help much, for extra wages will not mean more food but only more hats. They are all vivid, the hard, lucid daughters, the soft and illogical Mrs Heyham, and especially Mr Heyham, kindly, loving, generous, yet capable of every beastliness while maintaining his faith in his own rectitude. Mr Heyham is a triumph, for he is just everybody; he is 'the man with whose experiences women are trained to sympathise while he is not trained to sympathise with theirs.' He is the ordinary, desirous man, the male. Listen to this analysis of man: 'He has a need to impress himself on the world he finds outside him, an impulse that drives him to achieve his ends recklessly, ruthlessly, through any depth of suffering and conflict ... it is just by means of the qualities that are often so irritating, their tiresome restlessness, their curiosity, their disregard for security, for seemliness, even for life itself, that men have mastered the world and filled it with the wealth of civilisation. It is after this foolish, disorganised fashion of theirs, each of them—difficult, touchy creatures—busy with his personal ambitions, that they have armed the race with science, dignified it with art—one can take men lightly but one cannot take lightly the things that men have done.'

That sort of man sweats his waitresses because such is his duty to the shareholders. It is in this sort of man, Mr Heyham, who wants more money, in Edward Day, the prig who hates spending it, that Miss Amber Reeves realises herself. Analysis rather than evocation is her mission; she does not as a rule seek beauty, and when she strives, as in her last novel, Helen in Love, where a cheap little minx is kissed on the beach and is thus inspired, Miss Amber Reeves fails to achieve beauty in people; she achieves principally affectation. Beauty is not her metier; irony and pity are nearer to her, which is not so bad if we reflect that such is the motto of Anatole France. Oh! she is no mocking literary sprite, as the Frenchman, nor has she his graces; she is somewhat tainted by the seriousness of life, but she has this to distinguish her from her fellows: she can achieve laughter without hatred.

One should not, however, dismiss in a few words this latest novel. One can disregard the excellent picture of the lower-middle class family from which Helen springs, its circumscribed nastiness, its vulgar pleasure in appearances, for Miss Amber Reeves has done as good work before. But one must observe her new impulse towards the rich, idle, cultured people, whom she idealises so that they appear as worn ornaments of silver-gilt. It seems that she is reacting against indignation, that she is turning away from social reform towards the caste that has achieved a corner in graces. It may be that she has come to think the world incurable and wishes to retire as an anchorite ... only she retires to Capua: this is not good, for any withdrawal into a selected atmosphere implies that criticism of this atmosphere is suspended. Nothing so swiftly as that kills virility in literature.

But even so Miss Amber Reeves distinguishes herself from her immediate rivals, Miss Viola Meynell, Miss Bridget Maclagan, Miss Sheila Kaye-Smith, Miss Katherine Gerould, by an interest in business and in politics. She really knows what is a limited liability company or an issue warrant. She is not restricted to love, but embraces such problems as money, rank, science, class habits, which serve or destroy love. She finds her way in the modern tangle where emotion and cupidity trundle together on a dusty road. She is not always just, but she is usually judicial. Her men are rather gross instead of strong; she likes them, she tolerates them, they are altogether brutes and 'poor dears.' But then we are most of us a little like that.

3. SHEILA KAYE-SMITH

I do not know whether this is a compliment, but I should not be surprised if a reader of, say, Starbrace or Sussex Gorse, were to think that Sheila Kaye-Smith is the pen-name of a man. Just as one suspects those racy tales of guardsmen, signed 'Joseph Brown' or 'George Kerr,' of originating from some scented boudoir, so does one hesitate before the virility, the cognisance of oath and beer, of rotating crop, sweating horse, account book, vote and snickersnee that Sheila Kaye-Smith exhibits in all her novels. This is broader, deeper than the work of the women novelists of to-day, who, with the exception of Amber Reeves, are confined in a circle of eternally compounding pallid or purple loves. One side of her work, notably, surprises, and that is the direction of her thoughts away from women, their great and little griefs, towards men and the glory of their combat against fate. Sheila Kaye-Smith is more than any of her rivals the true novelist: the showman of life.

Yet she is a woman. You will imagine her as seeming small, but not so; very thin, with a grace all made of quiescence, her eyes gray and retracted a little, as if always in pain because man is not so beautiful as the earth that bore him, because he fails in idealism, falls away from his hopes and cannot march but only shamble from one eternity into another. There is in her a sort of cosmic choler restrained by a Keltic pride that is ready to pretend a world made up of rates and taxes and the 9.2 train to London Bridge. Afire within, she will not allow herself to 'commit melodrama.' In Isle of Thorns her heroine, Sally Odiarne, so describes her attempt to murder her lover, and I like to think of Sheila Kaye-Smith's will leashing the passion that strains. I like even more to think of the same will giving rein to anger, of a converse cry: 'Commit melodrama! I jolly well shall! I'm justabout sick of things!'

'Justabout!' That word, free-scattered in the speech of her rustics, is all Sussex. For Sheila Kaye-Smith has given expression to the county that from the Weald spreads green-breasted to meet the green sea. In all the novels is the slow Sussex speech, dotted with the kindly 'surelye,' the superlative 'unaccountable'; women are 'praaper,' ladies 'valiant,' troubles 'tedious.' It has colour, it is true English, unstained of Cockneyism and American. It is the speech of the oasthouse, of the cottage on the marsh, of the forester's hut in Udimore Wood, where sings the lark and rivulets flow like needles through the moss.

Assez de littérature! Sheila Kaye-Smith is not a painter, even though with dew diamonds the thorn-bush she spangle. Her Sussex is male: it is not the dessicated Sussex of the modern novelist, but the Sussex of the smuggler, of the Methodist, the squire; the Sussex where men sweat, and read no books. Old Sussex, and the Sussex of to-day which some think was created by the L.B. & S.C. Railway, she loves them both, and in both has found consolation, but I think she loves best the old. It was old Sussex made her first novel, The Tramping Methodist. Old Sussex bred its hero, Humphrey Lyte. He was a picaresque hero, the young rebel, for he grew enmeshed in murder and in love, in the toils of what England called justice in days when the Regent went to Brighton. But Lyte does not reveal Sheila Kaye-Smith as does Starbrace. Here is the apologia for the rebel: Starbrace, the son of a poor and disgraced man, will not eat the bread of slavery at his grandfather's price. You will imagine the old man confronted with this boy, of gentle blood but brought up as a labourer's son, hot, unruly, lusting for the freedom of the wet earth. Starbrace is a fool; disobedient he is to be flogged. He escapes among the smugglers on Winchelsea marsh, to the wild world of the mid-eighteenth century. It is a world of fighting, and of riding, of blood, of excisemen, of the 'rum pads' and their mistresses, their dicing and their death. Despite his beloved, Theodora Straightway, lady who fain would have him gentleman, Starbrace must ride away upon his panting horse, Pharisee. Love as he may, he cannot live like a rabbit in a hutch; he must have danger, be taken, cast into a cell, be released to die by the side of Pharisee, charging the Pretender's bodyguard at Prestonpans. All this is fine, for she has the secret of the historical novel: to show not the things that have changed, but those which have not.

Starbrace is, perhaps, Sheila Kaye-Smith's most brilliant flight, but not her most sustained. She has had other adventures in literature, such as Isle of Thorns, where Sally Odiarne wanders with Stanger's travelling show, hopelessly entangled in her loves, unable to seize happiness, unable to give herself to the tender Raphael, bound to good-tempered, sensual Andy, until at last she must kill Andy to get free, kill him to escape to the sea and die. But she finds God:—

'She had come out to seek death, and had found life. Who can stand against life, the green sea that tumbles round one's limbs and tears up like matchwood the breakwaters one has built? There, kneeling in the surf and spray, Sally surrendered to life.'

Sheila Kaye-Smith has not surrendered to life, though the weakness of her may be found in another book, Three Against the World, where the worthless Furlonger family can but writhe as worms drying in the sun; in the tired flatness of her last work, The Challenge to Sirius. The vagary of her mind is in such work as criticism: she has published a study of John Galsworthy which is judicial, though not inspired. But she was destined for finer tasks. Already in Spell Land, the story of a Sussex farm where lived two people, driven out of the village because they loved unwed, she had given a hint of her power to see not only man but the earth. She has almost stated herself in Sussex Gorse.

I have read many reviews of this book. I am tired of being told it is 'epic.' It is not quite; it has all the grace that Zola lacked in La Terre, but if the beauty is anything it is Virgilian, not Homeric. The scheme is immense, the life of Reuben Backfield, of Odiam, inspired in early youth with the determination to possess Boarzell, the common grown with gorse and firs, the fierce land of marl and shards where naught save gorse could live. The opening is a riot, for the Enclosures Act is in force and the squire is seizing the people's land. In that moment is born Reuben's desire; Boarzell shall be his. He buys some acres and his struggle is frightful; you see his muscles bulging in his blue shirt, you smell his sweat, you hear the ploughshare gripped with the stones, teeth biting teeth. For Boarzell Common is old, crafty, and savage, and would foil man. Reuben is not foiled; he can bear all things, so can dare all things. He buys more land; there shall be on his farm no pleasure so that he may have money to crush Boarzell. His brother, Harry, is struck while Reuben blows up the enemy trees, and haunts his life, a horrible, idiot figure; his wife, Naomi, ground down by forced child-bearing (for Boarzell needs men and Reuben sons) dies. His six sons, devoid of the money Boarzell takes, leave him; one becomes a thief, another a sailor, another a sot in London, another a success; all leave him, even his daughters; one to marry a hated rival farmer, one to love because Reuben forbade love, and to end on the streets. He loses all, he loses his pretty second wife, he loses Alice Jury whom alone he loved, he loses the sons that Rose gave him. He gives all to Boarzell, to fighting it for seventy years, sometimes victor, sometimes crushed, for Boarzell is evil and fierce:

'It lay in a great hush, a great solitude, a quiet beast of power and mystery. It seemed to call to him through the twilight like a love forsaken. There it lay: Boarzell—strong, beautiful, desired, untamed, still his hope, still his battle.'

There are faults, here and there, degraded clichés; Sheila Kaye-Smith loves the stars too well, and often indulges in horrid astronomic orgies; there is not enough actual combat with the earth; the author intervenes, points to the combat instead of leaving at grips the two beasts, Reuben and Boarzell. She has not quite touched the epic, yet makes us want to resemble the hero, fierce, cruel, but great when old and alone, still indomitable. And one wonders what she will do, what she will be. There are lines in her poems, Willow's Forge, that prophesy; the moment may be enough:—

'When the last constellations faint and fall, When the last planets burst in fiery foam, When all the winds have sunk asleep, when all The worn way-weary comets have come home— When past and present and the future flee, My moment lives!'

She may strive no more, as she proposes to the seeker in The Counsel of Gilgamesh:—

'Why wander round Gilgamesh? Why vainly wander round? What canst thou find, O seeker, Which hath not long been found?

What canst thou know, O scholar, Which hath not long been known? What canst thou have, O spoiler, Which dead men did not own?'

But I do not think so. I do not know whether she will be great. It is enough that to-day she is already alone.

Form and the Novel

Every now and then a reviewer, recovering the enthusiasm of a critic, discovers that the English novel has lost its form, that the men who to-day, a little ineffectually, bid for immortality, are burning the gods they once worshipped. They declare that the novel, because it is no longer a story travelling harmoniously from a beginning towards a middle and an end, is not a novel at all, that it is no more than a platform where self-expression has given place to self-proclamation. And sometimes, a little more hopefully, they venture to prophesy that soon the proud Sicambrian will worship the gods that he burnt.

I suspect that this classic revival is not very likely to come about. True, some writers, to-day in their cradles, may yet emulate Flaubert, but they will not be Flaubert. They may take something of his essence and blend it with their own; but that will create a new essence, for literature does not travel in a circle. Rather it travels along a cycloid, bending back upon itself, following the movement of man. Everything in the world we inhabit conspires to alter in the mirror of literature the picture it reflects; haste, luxury, hysterical sensuousness, race-optimism and race-despair. And notably publicity, the attitude of the Press. For the time has gone when novels were written for young ladies, and told the placid love of Edwin and Angeline; nowadays the novel, growing ambitious, lays hands upon science, commerce, philosophy: we write less of moated granges, more of tea-shops and advertising agencies, for the Press is teaching the people to look to the novel for a cosmic picture of the day, for a cosmic commentary.

Evidently it was not always so. Flaubert, de Maupassant, Butler, Tolstoy (who are not a company of peers), aspired mainly 'to see life sanely and to see it whole.' Because they lived in days of lesser social complexity, economically speaking, they were able to use a purely narrative style, the only notable living exponent of which is Mr Thomas Hardy. But we, less fortunate perhaps, confronted with new facts, the factory system, popular education, religious unrest, pictorial rebellion, must adapt ourselves and our books to the new spirit. I do not pretend that the movement has been sudden. Many years before L'Education Sentimentale was written, Stendhal had imported chaos (with genius) into the spacious 'thirties. But Stendhal was a meteor: Dostoievsky and Mr Romain Rolland had to come to break up the old narrative form, to make the road for Mr Wells and for the younger men who attempt, not always successfully, to crush within the covers of an octavo volume the whole of the globe spinning round its axis, to express with an attitude the philosophy of life, to preach by gospel rather than by statement.

Such movements as these naturally breed a reaction, and I confess that, when faced with the novels of the 'young men,' so turgid, so bombastic, I turn longing eyes towards the still waters of Turgenev, sometimes even towards my first influence, now long discarded—the novels of Zola. Though the Zeitgeist hold my hand and bid me abandon my characters, forget that they should be people like ourselves, living, loving, dying, and this enough; though it suggest to me that I should analyse the economic state, consider what new world we are making, enlist under the banner of the 'free spirits' or of the 'simple life,' I think I should turn again towards the old narrative simplicities, towards the schedules of what the hero said, and of what the vicar had in his drawing-room, if I were not conscious that form evolves.

If literature be at all a living force it must evolve as much as man, and more if it is to lead him; it must establish a correspondence between itself and the uneasy souls for which it exists. So it is no longer possible to content ourselves with such as Jane Austen; we must exploit ourselves. Ashamed as we are of the novel with a purpose, we can no longer write novels without a purpose. We need to express the motion of the world rather than its contents. While the older novelists were static, we have to be kinetic: is not the picture-palace here to give us a lesson and to remind us that the waxworks which delighted our grandfathers have gone?

But evolution is not quite the same thing as revolution. I do believe that revolution is only evolution in a hurry; but revolution can be in too great a hurry, and cover itself with ridicule. When the Futurists propose to suppress the adjective, the adverb, the conjunction, and to make of literature a thing of 'positive substantives' and 'dynamic verbs'—when Mr Peguy repeats over and over again the same sentence because, in his view, that is how we think—we smile. We are both right and wrong to smile, for these people express in the wrong way that which is the right thing. The modern novel has and must have a new significance. It is not enough that the novelist should be cheery as Dickens, or genially cynical as Thackeray, or adventurous as Fielding. The passions of men, love, hunger, patriotism, worship, all these things must now be shared between the novelist and his reader. He must collaborate with his audience ... emulate the show-girls in a revue, abandon the stage, and come parading through the stalls. A new passion is born, and it is a complex of the old passions; the novelist of to-day cannot end as Montaigne, say that he goes to seek a great perhaps. He needs to be more positive, to aspire to know what we are doing with the working-class, with the Empire, the woman question, and the proper use of lentils. It is this aspiration towards truth that breaks up the old form: you cannot tell a story in a straightforward manner when you do but glimpse it through the veil of the future.

And so it goes hard with Edwin and Angeline. We have no more time to tell that love; we need to break up their simple story, to consider whether they are eugenically fitted for each other, and whether their marriage settlement has a bearing upon national finance. Inevitably we become chaotic; the thread of our story is tangled in the threads which bind the loves of all men. We must state, moralise, explain, analyse motives, because we try to fit into a steam civilisation the old horse-plough of our fathers. I do not think that we shall break the old plough; now and then we may use it upon sands, but there is much good earth for it to turn.

There is always much talk of sincerity in literature. It is a favourite topic in literary circles, but often the argument sounds vain, for English literature seldom attains sincerity; it may never do so until Englishmen become Russians or Frenchmen, which, in spite of all temptations, they are not likely to do.

Once upon a time we had a scapegoat ready, the circulating libraries, for they made themselves ridiculous when they banned Black Sheep and The Uncounted Cost, while every now and then they have banned a book of artistic value, likely to lead astray the mothers rather than the daughters. Like the others, I foamed and fumed against the libraries, who after all were only conducting their business according to their commercial interests; like many others, I set up the idea that the circulating library was a sort of trustee for literature, and after this coronation I abused the library as one unworthy of a crown. It was rather unfair, for the conditions which militate against the free embodiment of brute facts into fiction form prevailed before the Library Censorship was thought of; the libraries have not made public opinion but followed it; nowadays they slightly influence it. For public opinion is not the opinion of the public, it is the opinion of a minority. The opinion of a minority makes the opinion of the majority, because the latter has, as a rule, no opinion at all.

Who the censorious minority is I do not quite know. I have a vision of a horrid conclave made up of the National Council of Public Morals, some shopkeepers addicted to their chapel in default of other vices, of anti-suffragists who think Ann Veronica dangerous; it must number some elderly ladies too, tired of converting the stubborn heathen, and I think some bishops, quite elderly and still more ladylike; there are celibates with whom celibacy has not agreed and who naturally want to serve out the world; there is everybody who in the name of duty, decency, self-control, purity, and such like catch-words, has stuffed his ears against the pipes of Pan with the cotton wool of aggressive respectability. A pretty congress, and like all congresses it talks as abundantly and as virulently as any young novelist. The vocal opinion of these people is well described in a recent successful revue: 'To the pure all things are impure.' Often of late years it has run amuck. Not long ago it caused the Municipal Libraries of Doncaster and Dewsbury to banish Tom Jones and to pronounce Westward Ho! unfit for devout Roman Catholics; it still spreads into the drama and holds such plays as Waste, Mrs Warren's Profession, Monna Vanna well hidden under the calico and red flannel of British rectitude; it has had its outbursts in picture palaces and music halls, where it happened to overlook the Salome dance and living pictures; often it unchains merriment, as on the perfect days when it cropped titles that seemed suggestive and caused plays to appear under more stimulating titles of 'The Girl Who Went' ... and 'The Girl Who Lost' ... (I do not remember what she lost, but I passionately want to know; such are the successes of Puritanism).

It is true that in some directions Puritanism has recently weakened. Plays long outcast, such as 'Damaged Goods,' 'Ghosts,' and 'The Three Daughters of Monsieur Dupont' have unashamedly taken the boards, but I fear that this does not exhibit the redemption of virtue by sin: if the newspapers had not conducted a campaign for the protection of the notoriously guileless New Zealand soldiers against the flapper with the hundred heads (every one of them filled with evil), if contagious diseases had not suddenly become fashionable, these plays would still be lying with the other unborn in the limbo of the Lord Chamberlain. But Puritanism has long teeth; it can still drive out of politics our next Charles Dilke, our next Parnell, however generous or gifted; it still hangs over the Law Courts, where women may be ordered out, or where cases may be heard in camera; it still holds some sway over everything but private life, where humanity recoups its public losses.

Puritan opinion has therefore a broader face of attack on the novel than is afforded by the Library Censorship. For the latter can injure a book but it cannot suppress it; on the whole banned books have suffered, but they have also benefited because many people buy what they cannot borrow, and because many buy the books which the Puritans advertise as unfit to read. (They are much disappointed, as a rule, unless they are themselves Puritans.) That buying class is not very large, but it counts, and I suppose we must charitably assume that the people who post to the bookseller to purchase the works which the library has rejected are supporters of literary sincerity; we must form our private opinion as to that. But whether the people who buy the banned book are or are not eager to obtain four-and-six penn'orth of truth, the fact remains that they do buy, that the deplorable authors do live, and that they do persist in writing their regrettable novels. The libraries have not killed sincerity; they have done no more than trammel it. For instance, in the well-known cases of The Devil's Garden, Sinister Street, and The Woman Thou Gavest Me, the faltering hesitation of the circulating libraries resulted in a colossal advertisement, of which Mr Maxwell and Mr Compton Mackenzie made the best, and Mr Hall Caine of course a little more. The libraries did not deprive of sustenance the authors of Limehouse Nights and Capel Sion, and in their new spirit did not interfere when Mr Galsworthy's heroine, in Beyond, made the best of one world and of two men.

The assassins of sincerity are the publisher and the policeman. Dismiss the illusion that banned books are bold and bad; for the most part they are kindly and mild, silly beyond the conception of Miss Elinor Glyn, beyond the sentimental limits of Mrs Barclay; they are seldom vicious in intent, and too devoid of skill to be vicious in achievement. The real bold books are unwritten or unpublished; for nobody but a fool would expect a publisher to be fool enough to publish them. There are, it is true, three or four London publishers who are not afraid of the libraries, but they are afraid of the police, and any one who wishes to test them can offer them, for instance, a translation of Le Journal d'une Femme de Chambre. A publisher is to a certain extent a human being; he knows that works of this type (and this one is masterly) are often works of art; he knows that they are saleable, and that assured profits would follow on publication, were the books not suppressed by the police. But he does not publish them, because he also knows that the police and its backers, purity societies and common informers, would demand seizure of the stock after the first review and hurry to Bow Street all those who had taken part in the printing and issue of the works. As a result many of these books are driven underground into the vile atmosphere of the vilest shops; some are great works of art; one is, in the words of Mr Anatole France, 'minded to weep over them with the nine Muses for company.' Need I say more than that Madame Bovary, the greatest novel the world has seen, is now being sold in a shilling paper edition under a cover which shows Madame Bovary in a sort of private dining-room, dressed in a chemise, and preparing to drink off a bumper of champagne. (Possibly the designer of this cover has in his mind sparkling burgundy.)

Several cases are fresh in my memory where purity, living in what Racine called 'the fear of God, sir, and of the police,' has intervened to stop the circulation of a novel. One is that of The Yoke, a novel of no particular merit, devoid of subversive teaching, but interesting because it was frank, because it did not portray love on the lines of musical comedy, because it faced the common sex problem of the middle aged spinster and the very young man, because it did not ignore the peril which everybody knows to be lurking within a mile of Charing Cross. The Yoke enjoyed a large sale at 6s. and was not interfered with, presumably because those who can afford 6s. may be abandoned to the scarlet woman. It was then published at a shilling. Soon after, the secret combination of common informer, purity group, and police forced the publisher into a police court, compelled him to express regret for the publication, and to destroy all the remaining copies and moulds. That is a brief tragedy, and it in no wise involves the library system. Another tragedy may be added. In 1910 Sudermann's novel, Das Hohe Lied, was published under the title of The Song of Songs. It is not a very interesting novel; it is long, rather crude, but it relates faithfully enough the career of a woman who lived by the sale of herself. The trouble was that she made rather a success of it, and it was shown in a few scenes that she did not always detest the incidents of this career, which is not unnatural. In December, 1910, two inspectors from the Criminal Investigation Department called on the publisher and informed his manager that a complaint had been made against the book; it was described as obscene. The officers apparently went on to say that their director, Sir Melville Macnaghten, did not associate himself with that opinion, but their object was to draw the publisher's attention to the fact that a complaint had been made. Thereupon, without further combat, the publisher withdrew the book. Nobody can blame him; he was not in business to fight battles of this kind, and I suppose that few British juries would have supported him. They would, more likely, have given the case against him first and tried to get hold of a private copy of the book after, presumably to read on Sunday afternoons. The interesting part of the business is that the accusation remained anonymous, that the police did not associate itself with it, but came humbly, helmet in hand, to convey the displeasure of some secret somebody with some secret something in the book. And there you are! That is all you need to snuff out the quite good work of a novelist with a quite good European reputation.

Once upon a time, I thought I might myself have a taste of the purity medicine. In 1910 I had ready for publication a novel called A Bed of Roses. I placed it with Messrs Alston Rivers, Ltd., whose standard of respectability was beyond attachment. They read the book without, so far as I remember, any ill effects; at least I saw no signs of corruption in the managing director and the secretary; the maidenly reserve of the lady shorthand-typist seemed unblemished. But some horrid internal convulsion must have suddenly occurred in the firm; they must have lost their nerve; or perhaps my corrupting influence was gradual and progressive; at any rate, they suddenly sent the book to their legal adviser, who wired back that it would almost certainly be prosecuted. So the contract was not signed, and if I had not, in those days, been an enthusiastic young man who longed to be prosecuted, I might never have published the book at all; the moral pressure might have been enough to keep it down. But I offered it to many publishers, all of whom rejected it, at the same time asking whether some milder spring might not be struck from the rock of my imagination, until I came across Mr Frank Palmer, who was a brave man. I offered him that book, cropped of about seventy pages, which I thought so true to life that I realised they must cause offence. He accepted it. Those were beautiful times, and I knew an exquisite day when I decided to chance the prosecution. I remember the bang of the MS. as it dropped into the post box; garbling an old song, I thought: 'Good-bye, good-bye, ye lovely young girls, we're off to Botany Bay.'

The police treated me very scurvily; they took no notice at all. The book was banned by all libraries owing to its alleged hectic qualities, and in due course achieved a moderate measure of scandalous success. I tell this story to show that had I been a sweet and shrinking soul, that if Mr Palmer had not shared in my audacity, the book would not have been published. We should not have been stopped, but we should have been frightened off, and this, I say, is the force that keeps down sincere novels, deep down in the muddy depths of their authors' imagination.

Now and then a publisher dares, and dares too far. Such is the case of The Rainbow, by Mr D. H. Lawrence, where the usual methods of Puritan terrorism were applied, where the publisher was taken into court, and made to eat humble pie, knowing that if he refused he must drink hemlock. Certainly The Rainbow was a bad book, for it was an ill-written book, a book of hatred and desire ... but many of us are people of hatred and desire, and I submit that there is no freedom when a minority of one in a nation of fifty millions is hampered in the expression of his feelings. More than one opinion has been held by one man and is now the belief of all the world. The beliefs of to-morrow will be slain if we suppress to-day the opinion of one. I would surrender all the rupees and virgins of Bengal for the sake of the atom of truth which may, in another age, build up immortal understanding in the heart of man.

All this has frightened publishers, so that they will now take no risks, and even the shy sincerity of English writers is turned away. The public subserve the Puritans, little mean people whom Mr Wells ideally nicknamed 'Key-hole,' or 'Snuffles,' little people who form 'watch committees' or 'vigilance societies'; who easily discover the obscene because it hangs like a film before their eyes, little people who keep the window shut. The police must obey, or be called corrupt; the courts are ready to apply the law severely rather than leniently, for who shall play devil's advocate at the Old Bailey? No wonder the publishers are frightened; the combination of their timidity, of truculent Puritanism and of a reluctantly vigilant police makes it almost impossible to publish a sincere work.

One result is that we are deprived of translations of foreign novels, some of which are of the first rank. There is Le Journal d'une Femme de Chambre; there is Aphrodite, the work of M. Pierre Louys, who is an artist in his way; there is Mr Boylesve's delicate, inwrought La Leçon d'Amour dans un Parc; there is the Parisian mischief of M. Prévost's Lettres de Femmes, the elegance of M. Henri de Régnier. Sanin got through, how I do not know; I have not read the translation, and it may very well be that it escaped only after the translator had thickly coated it with the soapsuds of English virtue.

Small as their chances may be it is a pity that the publishers do not adventure. It is true that Mr Vizetelly went to jail for publishing translations of Zola's novels, but when we are told by Mr George Moore that Mr W. T. Stead confided to him that the Vigilance Society considered the prosecution of Madame Bovary, it seems necessary again to test the law. For you will observe that in all the cases quoted the publisher has not allowed himself to be committed for trial; he has chosen the prudent and humble course of apologising and withdrawing the book, and one wonders what would happen if just once, supported by a common fund, a publisher were to face the Puritans, let the case go for trial, test the law. One wonders what the result might not be in the hands of, for instance, Sir John Simon. He might win a glorious victory for English letters; he might do away with much of the muckraking which is keeping English letters in subjection because nobody dares drag it out for public exposure and combat. Until that happens Puritan influence is more potent than a score of convictions, for no publisher knows what he may do and what he may not; prosecution is as effective in threat as in action, and I hope that if ever this struggle comes it will be over some book of mine.

Let it be clear that no blame attaches to the publisher; he does not trade under the name 'Galahad & Co.'; he knows that even defeated Puritans would attempt to avenge their downfall, and malignantly pursue all the works he issued in every municipal library. But still it is a pity that no publisher will face them; half a dozen of our best known publishers are knights: perhaps one day one of them will put on his armour.

This secret terrorism is a national calamity, for it procures the sterilisation of the English novel. It was always so, for there is not complete sincerity in Tom Jones, or in A Mummer's Wife, even as the word sincerity is understood in England, and there is little nowadays. We have to-day a certain number of fairly courageous novelists whose works are alluded to in other chapters, but they are not completely sincere. If they were they would not be concerned with censorships; they would not be published at all. I do not suggest that they wish to be insincere, but they cannot help it. Their insincerity, I suspect, as exemplified by the avoidance of certain details, arises from the necessity of that avoidance; it arises also from the habit of concealment and evasion which a stupefied public, led by a neurotic faction, has imposed upon them.

Our novelists openly discuss every feature of social life, politics, religion, but they cast over sex a thick veil of ellipse and metaphor. Thus Mr Onions suggests, but dares not name, the disease a character contracts; Mr Lawrence leaves in some doubt the actual deeds of his Trespasser, while 'H. H. Richardson' leaves to our conjectures the habits of Schilsky. (So do I, you see; if I were to say exactly what I mean it would never do.)

It may be said that all this is not insincerity, and that there is no need to dwell upon what the respectable call the unwholesome, the unhealthy, the unnecessary, but I think we must accept that the bowdlerising to which a novelist subjects his own work results in lopsidedness. If a novelist were to develop his characters evenly the three hundred page novel might extend to five hundred; the additional two hundred pages would be made up entirely of the sex preoccupations of the characters, their adventures and attempts at satisfaction. There would be as many scenes in the bedroom as in the drawing-room, probably more, given that human beings spend more time in the former than in the latter apartment. There would be abundant detail, detail that would bring out an intimacy of contact, a completeness of mutual understanding which does not generally come about when characters meet at breakfast or on the golf course. The additional pages would offer pictures of the sex side of the characters, and thus would compel them to come alive; at present they often fail to come alive because they develop only on, say, five sides out of six.

No character in a modern English novel has been fully developed. Sometimes, as in the case of Mendel, of Jude the Obscure, of Mark Lennan, of Gyp Fiörsen, one has the impression that they are fully developed because the book mainly describes their sex adventures, but one could write a thousand pages about sex adventures and have done nothing but produce sentimental atmosphere. A hundred kisses do not make one kiss, and there is more truth in one page of Madame Bovary, than in the shackled works of Mr Hardy. It is not his fault, it is a case of ... if England but knew ... and, therefore, if Hardy but could. Our literary characters are lopsided because their ordinary traits are fully portrayed, analysed with extraordinary minuteness, while their sex life is cloaked, minimised, or left out. Therefore, as the ordinary man does indulge his sexual proclivities, as a large proportion of his thoughts run on sex, if he is a live man, the characters in modern novels are false. They are megacephalous and emasculate. If their religious views, their political opinions, their sporting tastes were whittled down as cruelly as their sexual tendencies, then the characters would become balanced; they would be dwarfs, but they would be true; if all the characteristics of men were as faintly suggested in them as their sexual traits, the persons that figure in novels would simulate reality.

They would not be reality, but they would be less untrue than they are to-day. This, however, is merely theory, for it is impossible to apply to the novel the paradox that insincerity in everything being better than insincerity in one thing it is desirable to be insincere throughout. The paradox cannot be applied, because then a novel of ideas could not be written; shrouded religious doubt, shy socialism, suggested anarchism, would reduce the length by nine tenths, make of the novel a short story. It would be perfectly balanced and perfectly insincere; aesthetically sound, it would satisfy nobody. We should be compelled to pad it out with murder, theft, and arson, which, as everybody knows, are perfectly moral things to write about.

It is a cruel position for the English novel. The novelist may discuss anything but the main pre-occupation of life. If he describes the City clerk he may dilate upon City swindles, but he must select warily from among the City clerk's loves. The novelist knows these loves, records them in his mind, speaks of them freely, but he does not write them down. If he did, his publisher would go to jail. For this reason there is no completely sincere writing. The novelist is put into the witness box, but he is not sworn to tell the truth, the whole truth and nothing but the truth; he is sworn to tell the truth, but not the whole truth. He is not perjured, but he is muzzled.

Obviously this is an unhealthy state, for the spirit of a people is in its books, and I suspect that it does a people no good if its preoccupation find no outlet; it develops inhibitions, while its Puritan masters develop phobias. The cloaking of the truth makes neither modesty nor mock modesty; it makes impurity. There is no market for pornography, for pornography makes no converts who were not already converted. I believe that the purity propaganda creates much of the evil that lives; I charge advertising reformers with minds full of hate, bishops full of wind, and bourgeois full of fear, with having exercised through the pulpit and the platform a more stimulating effect upon youth, and with having given it more unhealthy information about white slavery, secret cinemas, and disorderly houses than it could ever have gained from all the books that were ever printed in Amsterdam. I once went to a meeting for men only, and came out with two entirely new brands of vice; a bishop held up to me the luridities of secret cinemas, and did everything for me except to give me the address. But he filled my mind with cinemas. One could multiply these instances indefinitely. I do not think that we should cover things up; we had enough of that during the mid-Victorian period, when respectability was at its height, and when women, in bodice and bustle, did their best to make respectability difficult; no, we do not want things covered up, but we do want them advertised. I believe that as good coin drives out bad the Puritans would find a greater safety and the world a greater freedom in allowing good literature to vie with evil; the good would inevitably win; no immoral literature is good; all bad literature dies. The seventeenth and eighteenth centuries in England and France produced the vilest pornography we know. Those centuries also produced Molière and Fielding. Well, to-day, you can buy Molière and Fielding everywhere, but the pornography of those centuries is dead, and you can find it nowhere except in a really good West End club.

It may be argued that the English are not, as a nation, interested in sex, that they do not discuss it and that they do not think about it. If this were true, then a novelist would be sincere if he devoted nine tenths of his novel to business and play and no more than a tenth to sex. But it is not true. The English, particularly English women, speak a great deal about sex and, as they are certainly shy of the subject, they must devote to it a great deal of thought which they never put into words. If anybody doubts this, let him play eavesdropper in a club, a public house, or an office, listen to men, their views, their stories; let him especially discover how many 'humorous' tales are based on sex. And let him discreetly ascertain the topics young women discuss when no men are present; some, like Elsie Lindtner, are frank enough to tell.

In their private lives the English do not talk of sex as they would like to, but they do talk, and more openly every day. Yet their sex preoccupations are not reflected in the novels which purport to reflect their lives; conversation is over-sexed, the novel is under-sexed, therefore untrue, therefore insincere. For this there is no immediate remedy. Neither the Society of Authors, nor a combine of publishers, nor a 'Liberty Library' can shake the combination of fears which actuates persecution. The law should certainly be tested, just as it was tested in France by the prosecution of Flaubert in 1857, but we know perfectly well that even a victory for sincerity would do no more than carry us a little nearer to our goal. The law is a trifle compared with public feeling, and public feeling is a trifle beside the emotions the public is told it ought to feel. We had best reconcile ourselves to the inevitable, admit that we cannot be sincere because the police dare not allow it, and acquit the libraries of this one sin, that they killed in English literature a sincerity which was not there.

1. TARTARIN

It is not every country and every period gives birth to a comic giant. Tragic and sentimental heroes are common, and make upon the history of literature a mark of sorts; we have Achilles and Werther, William Tell, d'Artagnan, Tristan, Sir Galahad, others, too, with equal claims to fame: but comic giants are few. The literature of the world is full of comic pigmies; it is fairly rich in half-growns such as Eulenspiegel, Mr Dooley, Tchitchikoff, and Mr Pickwick, but it does not easily produce the comic character who stands alone and massive among his fellows, like Balzac among novelists. There are not half a dozen competitors for the position, for Pantagruel and Gargantua are too philosophic, while Don Quixote does not move every reader to laughter; he is too romantic, too noble; he is hardly comic. Baron von Münchausen, Falstaff, and Tartarin alone remain face to face, all of them simple, all of them adventurous, but adventurous without literary inflation, as a kitten is adventurous when it explores a work-basket. There is no gigantic quality where there is self-consciousness or cynicism; the slightest strain causes the gigantic to vanish, the creature becomes human. The comic giant must be obvious, he must be, to himself, rebellious to analysis; he must also be obvious to the beholder, indeed transparent. That is not a paradox, it is a restatement of the fact that the comic giant's simplicity must be so great that everybody but he will realise it.

All this Tartarin fulfils. He is the creature of Alphonse Daudet, a second-rate writer who has earned for him a title maybe to immortality. There is no doubt that Daudet was a second-rate writer, and that Mr George Moore was right when he summed him up as de la bouillabaisse; his novels are sentimental, his reminiscences turgid, his verses suitable for crackers, but Daudet had an asset—his vivid feeling for the South. It was not knowledge or observation made Tartarin; it was instinct. Neither in Tartarin de Tarascon nor in Tartarin sur les Alpes was Daudet for a moment inconsistent or obscure; for him, Tartarin and his followers stood all the time in violent light. He knew not only what they had to say in given circumstances, but also what they would say in any circumstances that might arise.

It is not wonderful then, that Tartarin appears as a large character. You will figure him throughout as a French bourgeois, aged about forty in the first novel, fifty in the second, and sixty in the third. Daudet's dates being unreliable, you must assume his adventures as happening between 1861 and 1881, and bridge the gaps that exist between them with a vision of Tartarin's stormily peaceful life in the sleepy town of Tarascon. For Tartarin was too adventurous to live without dangers and storms. When he was not shooting lions in Algeria, or climbing the Alps, or colonising in Polynesia, Tartarin was still a hero: he lived in his little white house with the green shutters, surrounded with knives, revolvers, rifles, double-handed swords, crishes, and yataghans; he read, not the local paper, but Fenimore Cooper and Captain Cook; he learned how to fight and how to hunt, how to follow a trail, or he hypnotised himself with the recitals of Alpine climbs, of battles in China with the bellicose Tartar. Save under compulsion, he never did anything, partly because there was nothing to do at Tarascon, partly because his soul was turned rather towards bourgeois comfort than towards glory and blood. This, however, the fiery Southerner could not accept: if he could not do he could pretend, and thus did Daudet establish the enormous absurdity of his character.

There was nothing to shoot at Tarascon, so Tartarin and his followers went solemnly into the fields and fired at their caps; there was nothing to climb, except the neighbouring Alpilles ... whose height was three hundred feet, but Tartarin bought an alpen-stock and printed upon his visiting-cards initials which meant 'President of the Alpine Club'; there was no danger in the town, but Tartarin never went out at night without a dagger and several guns. He was a bourgeois, but he was a romantic: he had to find in fiction the excitement that life refused him, to create it where it did not exist. In the rough, Tartarin was the jovial Frenchman of the South, short, fat, excitable, unable to see things as they are, unable to restrain his voice, his gestures, his imagination; he was greedy and self-deceived, he saw trifles as enormous, he placed the world under a magnifying glass.

Because of this enormous vision of life Tartarin was driven into adventure. Because he magnified his words he was compelled by popular opinion to sail to Algiers to shoot lions, though he was at heart afraid of dogs; to scale the Alps, though he shuddered when he thought of catching cold. He had to justify himself in the eyes of his fellow-citizens, or forgo for ever the halo of heroism. He did not have to abandon it, for Daudet loved his Tartarin; in Algeria he was mocked, swindled, beaten, but somehow he secured his lion's skin; and, in the Alps, he actually scaled both the Jungfrau and Mont Blanc ... the first without knowing that it was dangerous, the second against his will. Tartarin won because he was vital, his vitality served him as a shield. All his qualities were of those that make a man absurd but invincible; his exaggeration, his histrionics, his mock heroics, his credulity, his mild sensuality, his sentimentality, and his bumptious cowardice—all this blended into an enormous bubbling charm which neither man nor circumstance could in the end withstand.

Daudet brings out his traits on every page. Everywhere he makes Tartarin strut and swell as a turkey-cock. Exaggeration, in other words lying, lay in every word and deed of Tartarin. He could not say: 'We were a couple of thousand at the amphitheatre yesterday,' but naturally said: 'We were fifty thousand.' And he was not exactly lying; Daudet, who loved him well, pleaded that this was not lying but mirage, mirage induced by the hot sun. He was not quite wrong: when Tartarin said that he had killed forty lions he believed it; and his fellow-climber believed the absurd story he had concocted: that Switzerland was a fraud, that there were eiderdowns at the bottom of every crevasse, and that he had himself climbed the Andes on his hands and knees. Likewise, Tartarin and the people of Tarascon were deceived by their own histrionics. The baobab (arbos gigantea) which Tartarin trained in a flower-pot stood, in their imagination, a hundred feet high.

Histrionics and mock heroics pervade the three books. It is not the fact that matters, it is the fact seen through the coloured Southern mind, and that mind turns at once away from the fact towards the trifles that attend it. Thus costume is everywhere a primary concern. Tartarin cannot land at Algiers to shoot lions unless he be dressed for the part in Arab clothes, and he must carry three rifles, drag behind him a portable camp, a pharmacy, a patent tent, patent compressed foods. Nothing is too absurd for him: he has a 'Winchester rifle with thirty-two cartridges in the magazine'; he does not shrink from a rifle with a semicircular barrel for shooting round the corner. To climb the Righi (instead of using the funicular) he must wear a jersey, ice-shoes, snow goggles. Everywhere he plays a part and plays it in costume. Nor is Tartarin alone in this; the Tarasconnais emulate their chief: Major Bravida dons black when he calls to compel Tartarin 'to redeem his honour' and sail for Algiers; when Port Tarascon, the frantic colony, is formed, costumes are designed for grandees, for the militia, for the bureaucrats. Appearances alone matter: Tarascon is not content with the French flag, but spread-eagles across it a fantastic local animal, La Tarasque, of mythical origin.

Life in Tarascon is too easy: Tartarin helps it on with a war-whoop. He creates adventure. Thus in 1870 he organises against the Germans the defence of the town; mines are laid under the marketplace, the Café de la Comédie is turned into a redoubt, volunteers drill in the street. Of course there is no fighting, the Germans do not come, nor do the prudent Tarasconnais attempt to seek them out, but in its imagination the town has been heroic. It is heroic again when it defends against the Government the monks of Pampérigouste: the convent becomes a fortress, but there is no fighting; when the supplies give out the heroic defenders march out with their weapons and their banners, in their crusaders' uniforms. The town believes. It believes anything and anybody. Because a rogue calls himself a prince, Tartarin entrusts him with his money and is deserted in the Sahara; because another calls himself a duke, thousands of Tarasconnais follow Tartarin to a non-existent colony bought by them from the pseudo-duke. Whether the matter be general or personal Tartarin believes. He falls in love with a Moorish girl, and innocently allows himself to be persuaded that a substitute is the beauty whom he glimpsed through the yashmak.

Tartarin believes because he is together romantic, sentimental, and mildly sensual: that which he likes he wants to think true. He wants to believe that sweet Baia is his true love; when again he succumbs to Sonia, the Russian exile, he wants to believe that he too is an extremist, a potential martyr in the cause of Nihilism; and again he wants to believe that Likiriki, the nigger girl, is the little creature of charm for whom his heart has been calling. His sentimentality is always ready—for women, for ideas, for beasts. He can be moved when he hears for the hundredth time the ridiculous ballads that are popular in the local drawing-rooms, weep when Bezuquet, the chemist, sings 'Oh thou, beloved white star of my soul!' For him the lion is 'a noble beast,' who must be shot, not caged; the horse 'the most glorious conquest of man.' He is always above the world, never of it unless his own safety be endangered, when he scuttles to shelter; as Daudet says, half Tartarin is Quixote, half is Sancho ... but Sancho wins. It is because Tartarin is a comic coward that he will not allow the heroic crusaders of Pampérigouste to fire on the Government troops; the 'abbot' of Port Tarascon to train the carronade on the English frigate; alone, he is a greater coward than in public; he shivers under his weapons when he walks to the club in the evening; he severs the rope on Mont Blanc, sending his companion to probable death. But the burlesque does not end tragically: nobody actually dies, all return to Tarascon in time to hear their funeral orations.

It might be thought that Tartarin is repulsive: he is not; he is too young, too innocent. His great, foolish heart is too open to the woes of any damsel; his simplicity, his credulity, his muddled faith, the optimism which no misfortune can shatter—all these traits endear him to us, make him real. For Tartarin is real: he is the Frenchman of the South; in the words of a character, 'The Tarasconnais type is the Frenchman magnified, exaggerated, as seen in a convex mirror.' Tartarin and his fellows typify the South, though some typify one side of the Southern Frenchman rather than another; thus Bravida is military pride, Excourbaniès is the liar, and mild Pascalon is the imitator of imitators: when Tarascon, arrested by the British captain and brought home on board the frigate, takes up the attitude of Napoleon on the Bellerophon, Pascalon begins a memorial and tries to impersonate Las Cases. As for Tartarin, bell-wether of the flock, he has all the characteristics, he even sings all the songs. He is the South.

The three Tartarin books constitute together the most violent satire that has ever been written against the South. Gascony, Provence, and Languedoc are often made the butts of Northern French writers, while Lombards introduce in books ridiculous Neapolitans, and Catalonians paint burlesque Andalusians, but no writer has equalled Alphonse Daudet in consistent ferocity. So evident is this, that Tarascon to this day resents the publications, and that, some years ago, a commercial traveller who humorously described himself on the hotel register as 'Alphonse Daudet' was mobbed in the street, and rescued by the police from the rabble who threatened to throw him into the Rhone. Tarascon, a little junction on the way to Marseilles, has been made absurd for ever. Yet, though Daudet exaggerated, he built on the truth: there is a close connection between his preposterous figures, grown men with the tendencies of children enormously distorted, and the Frenchmen of the South. Indeed, the Southern Frenchman is the

Frenchman as we picture him in England; there is between him and his compatriot from Picardy or Flanders a difference as great as exists between the Scotsman and the man of Kent. The Northern Frenchman is sober, silent, hard, reasonable, and logical; his imagination is negligible, his artistic taste as corrupt as that of an average inhabitant of the Midlands. But the Southern Frenchman is a different creature; his excitable temperament, his irresponsibility and impetuousness run through the majority of French artists and politicians. As the French saying goes, 'the South moves'; thus it is not wonderful that Le Havre and Lille should not rival Marseilles and Bordeaux.

Tartarin lives to a greater or lesser degree within every Frenchman of the plains, born South of the line which unites Lyons and Bordeaux. It is Tartarin who stands for hours at street corners in Arles or Montpellier, chattering with Tartarin and, like Tartarin, endlessly brags of the small birds he has killed, of the hearts he has won and of his extraordinary luck at cards. It is Tartarin again who still wears night-caps and flannel belts, and drinks every morning great bowls of chocolate. And it is Tartarin who, light-heartedly, joins the colonial infantry regiment and goes singing into battle because he likes the adventure and would rather die in the field than be bored in barracks. Daudet has maligned the South so far as courage is concerned: there is nothing to show that the Southerners, Tarasconnais and others, are any more cowardly than the men of the North. Courage goes in zones, and because the North has generally proved harder the South must not be indicted en bloc. Presumably Daudet felt compelled to make Tartarin a poltroon so as to throw into relief his braggadocio; that is a flaw in his work, but if it be accepted as the licence of a litterateur, it does not mar the picture of Tartarin.

It should not, therefore, be lost sight of by the reader of Tartarin de Tarascon and of Tartarin Sur Les Alpes that this is a caricature. Every line is true, but modified a little by the 'mirage' that Alphonse Daudet so deftly satirises; it is only so much distorted as irony demands. Tartarin de Tarascon is by far the best of the three books; it is the most compact, and within its hundred-odd pages the picture of Tartarin is completely painted; the sequel is merely the response of the author to the demand of a public who so loved Tartarin as to buy five hundred thousand copies of his adventures. As for Port Tarascon, the beginning of Tartarin's end, it should not have been written, for it closes on a new Tartarin who no longer believes in his own triumphs—a sober, disillusioned Tartarin, shorn of his glory, flouted by his compatriots and ready to die in a foreign town. Alphonse Daudet had probably tired of his hero, for he understood him no longer. The real Tartarin could not be depressed by misadventure, chastened by loss of prestige: to cast him to earth could only bring about once more the prodigy of Anteus. He would have risen again, more optimistic and bombastic than ever, certain that no enemy had thrown him and that he had but slipped. And if Tartarin had to die, which is not certain, for Tartarin's essence is immortal, he could not die disgraced, but must die sumptuously—like Cleopatra among her jewels, or a Tartar chief standing on his piled arms on the crest of a funeral pyre.

2. FALSTAFF

Like Hamlet, Tartuffe, Don Quixote, Falstaff has had his worshippers and his exegetists. The character Dr. Johnson dwelled on still serves to-day to exercise the critical capacity of the freshman; he is one of the stars in a crowded cast, a human, fallible, lovable creature, and it is not wonderful that so many have asked themselves whether there lurked fineness and piety within his gross frame. But, though 'his pyramid rise high unto heaven,' it is not everybody has fully realised his psychological enormity, his nationality; the tendency has been to look upon him rather as a man than as a type. I do not contend that it is desirable to magnify type at the expense of personality; far from it, for the personal quality is ever more appealing than the typical, but one should not ignore the generalities which hide in the individual, especially when they are evident. It is remarkable that Dr Johnson should have so completely avoided this side of Falstaff's character, so remarkable that I quote in full his appreciation of the fat Knight[5]:—

[5: Following on the second part of King Henry IV., Dr Johnson's edition, 1765.]

'But Falstaff, unimitated, unimitable Falstaff! how shall I describe thee? thou compound of sense and vice; of sense which may be admired, but not esteemed; of vice which may be despised, but hardly detested. Falstaff is a character loaded with faults, and with those faults which naturally produce contempt. He is a thief and a glutton, a coward and a boaster; always ready to cheat the weak, and prey upon the poor; to terrify the timorous, and insult the defenceless. At once obsequious and malignant, he satirises in their absence those whom he lives by flattering. He is familiar with the prince only as an agent of vice; but of this familiarity he is so proud, as not only to be supercilious and haughty with common men, but to think his interest of importance to the Duke of Lancaster. Yet the man thus corrupt, thus despicable, makes himself necessary to the prince that despises him, by the most pleasing of all qualities, perpetual gaiety; by an unfailing power of exciting laughter, which is the more freely indulged, as his wit is not of the splendid or ambitious kind, but consists in easy scapes and sallies of levity, which make sport, but raise no envy. It must be observed, that he is stained with no enormous or sanguinary crimes, so that his licentiousness is not so offensive but that it may be borne for his mirth.'

A judgment such as this one is characteristic of Johnson; it is elaborate, somewhat prejudiced, and very narrow. Johnson evidently saw Falstaff as a mere man, perhaps as one whose ghost he would willingly have taught to smoke a churchwarden at the 'Cheshire Cheese.' He saw in him neither heroic nor national qualities and would have scoffed at the possibility of their existence, basing himself on his own remark to Boswell: 'I despise those who do not see that I am right....'

But smaller men than Johnson have judged Falstaff in a small way. They have concentrated on his comic traits, and considered very little whether he might be dubbed either giant or Englishman: if Falstaff is a diamond they have cut but one or two facets. Now the comic side of Falstaff must not be ignored; if he were incapable of creating laughter, if he could draw from us no more than a smile, as do the heroes of Anatole France, of Sterne, or Swift, his gigantic capacity would be affected. It is essential that he should be absurd; it is almost essential that he should be fat, for it is an established fact that humanity laughs gladly at bulk, at men such as Sancho Panza and Mr Pickwick. It is likely that Shakespeare was aware of our instinct when he caused Hal to call Falstaff 'this bed-presser, this horseback-breaker, this huge hill of flesh.' In the mathematics of the stage fat = comedy, lean = tragedy; I do not believe that Hamlet was flesh-burdened, even though 'scant of breath.'

Fat was, however, but Falstaff's prelude to comedy. He needed to be what he otherwise was, coarse, salaciously-minded, superstitious, blustering, cowardly, and lying; he needed to be a joker, oft-times a wit, and withal a sleepy drunkard, a butt for pranks. His coarseness is comic, but not revolting, for it centres rather on the human body than on the human emotion; he does not habitually scoff at justice, generosity or faithfulness, even though he be neither just, nor generous, nor faithful: his brutality is a brutality of word rather than thought, one akin to that of our poorer classes. Had Falstaff not had an air of the world and a custom of courts he would have typified the lowest classes of our day and perhaps stood below those of his own time. His is the coarseness of the drunkard, a jovial and not a maudlin drunkard; when sober he reacts against his own brutality, vows to '... purge and leave sack, and live cleanly, as a nobleman should do.'

Falstaff led his life by a double thread. Filled with the joy of living, as he understood it, limited by his desires for sack and such as Doll Tearsheet, he was bound too by his stupidity. He was stupid, though crafty, as is a cat, an instinctive animal; none but a stupid man could have taken seriously the mockery of the fairies in Windsor Park; himself it is acknowledges that he is 'made an ass.' We laugh, and again we laugh when, in silly terror and credulity, he allows the Merry Wives to pack him in the foul linen basket; where Falstaff is, there is also rubicund pleasantry.

In the same spirit we make merry over his cowardice; the cowardice itself is not comic, indeed it would be painful to see him stand and deliver to Gadshill, if the surrender were not prefaced by the deep grumbles of a man who suspects that Hal and Poins have captured his affections with drugs, who acknowledge that 'eight yards of uneven ground is threescore and ten miles afoot' with him. The burlesque conceals the despicable, and we fail to sneer because we laugh; we forgive his acceptance of insult at the hands of the Chief Justice's servant: it is not well that a knight should allow a servant to tell him that he lies in his throat, but if leave to do so can be given in jest the insult loses its sting. Falstaff is more than a coward, he is the coward-type, for he is (like Pistol) the blustering coward. The mean, cringing coward is unskilled at his trade: the true coward is the fat knight who, no sooner convicted of embellishing his fight with highwaymen, of having forgone his booty rather than defend it, can roar that he fears and will obey no man, and solemnly say: "Zounds! an' I were at the strappado, or all the racks in the world, I would not tell you upon compulsion.' The attitude is so simple, so impudent, that we laugh, forgive. And we forgive because such an attitude could not be struck with confidence save by a giant.

A giant he is, this comic and transparent man. There is nothing unobtrusive in Falstaff's being; his feelings and his motives are large and unmistakable. His jolly brutality and mummery of pride are in themselves almost enough to ensure him the crown of Goliath, but add to these the poetry wrapped in his lewdness, the idealistic gallantry which follows hard upon his crudity, add that he is lawless because he is adventurous, add simplicity, bewilderment, and cast over this temperament a web of wistful philosophy: then Falstaff stands forth enormous and alone.

Falstaff is full of gross, but artistic glee; for him life is epic and splendid, and his poetic temperament enables him to discover the beauty that is everywhere. It may be that Henry IV. rightly says: 'riot and dishonour stain the brow of my young Harry,' but it may be also that the young prince is not unfortunate in a companion who can find grace in highwaymen: '... let us not that are squires of the night's body be called thieves of the day's beauty: let us be Diana's foresters, gentlemen of the shade, minions of the moon; and let men say, we be men of good government, being governed as the sea is, by our noble and chaste mistress the moon, under whose countenance we steal.' Falstaff is big with the love of life and ever giving birth to it; he is the spirit of the earth, a djinn released whom none may bottle. Because of this he is lawless; he cannot respect the law, for he can respect no limits; he bursts out from the small restrictions of man as does his mighty paunch from his leather belt. It is hopeless to try to abash him; force even, as embodied in the Chief Justice, does not awe him overmuch, so well does he know that threats will not avail to impair his pleasure. Falstaff in jail would make merry with the jailers, divert them with quips, throw dice and drink endlessly the sack they would offer him for love. He cannot be daunted, feeling too deeply that he holds the ball of the world between his short arms; once only does Falstaff's big, gentle heart contract, when young Hal takes ill his kindly cry: 'God save thee, my sweet boy!' He is assured that he will be sent for in private, and it is in genuine pain rather than fear he cries out: 'My lord, my lord!' when committed to the Fleet.

In this simple faith lies much of Falstaff's gigantic quality. To believe everything, to be gullible, in brief to be as nearly as may be an instinctive animal, that is to be great. I would not have Falstaff sceptical; he must be credulous, faithfully become the ambassador of Ford to Ford's wife, and be deceived, and again deceived; he must believe himself loved of all women, of Mistress Ford, or Mistress Page, or Doll Tearsheet; he must readily be fooled, pinched, pricked, singed, ridiculously arrayed in the clothes of Mother Prat. One moment of doubt, a single inquiry, and the colossus would fall from his pedestal, become as mortal and suspicious men. But there is no downfall; he believes and, breasting through the sea of ridicule, he holds Mistress Ford in his arms for one happy moment, the great moment which even a rain of potatoes from the sky could not spoil. It could not, for there echoes in Falstaff's mind the sweet tune of 'Green Sleeves':

'Greensleeves was all my joy, Greensleeves was my delight, Greensleeves was my heart of gold, And who but Lady Greensleeves?'

It is natural that such a temperament should, in the ordinary sense, breed lies. Falstaff does and does not lie; like Tartarin he probably suffers from mirage and, when attacked by highwaymen, truly sees them as a hundred when, in fact, they are but two. But he is not certain, he is too careless of detail, he readily responds when it is suggested he lies and makes the hundred into a mere sixteen. Falstaff the artist is either unconscious of exaggeration, therefore truthful, or takes a childish pleasure in exaggerating; he is a giant, therefore may exaggerate, for all things are small relatively to him. If the ocean could speak none would reproach it if it said that fifty inches of rain had fallen into its bosom within a single hour, for what would it matter? one inch or fifty, what difference would that make to the ocean? Falstaff is as the ocean; he can stand upon a higher pedestal of lies than can the mortal, for it does not make him singular. Indeed it is this high pedestal of grossness, lying, and falsity makes him great; no small man would dare to erect it; Falstaff dares, for he is unashamed.

He is unashamed, and yet not quite unconscious. I will not dilate on the glimmerings that pierce through the darkness of his vanity: if anything they are injurious, for they drag him down to earth; Shakespeare evidently realised that these glimmerings made Falstaff more human, introduced them with intention, for he could not know that he was creating a giant, a Laughter God, who should be devoid of mortal attributes. But these flecks are inevitable, and perhaps normal in the human conception of the extra-human: the Greek Gods and Demigods, too, had their passions, their envies, and their tantrums. Falstaff bears these small mortalities and bears them easily with the help of his simple, sincere philosophy.

It is pitiful to think of Falstaff's death, in the light of his philosophy. According to Mr Rowe,[6] 'though it be extremely natural, "it" is yet as diverting as any part of his life.' I do not think so, for hear Mrs Quickly, the wife of Pistol: 'Nay, sure, he's not in hell: he's in Arthur's bosom, if ever man went to Arthur's bosom. A' made a finer end, and went away, an it had been any christom child; a' parted just between twelve and one, even at the turning o' the tide: for after I saw him fumble with the sheets, and play with flowers, and smile upon his fingers' ends, I knew there was but one way; for his nose was as sharp as a pen, and a' babbled of green fields. "How now, Sir John!" quoth I: "what, man! be of good cheer!" So a' cried out, "God, God, God!" three or four times: now I, to comfort him, bid him a' should not think of God; I hoped there was no need to trouble himself with any such thoughts yet. So a' bade me lay more clothes on his feet; I put my hand into the bed, and felt them, and they were as cold as any stone; then I felt to his knees, and so upward, and upward, and all was as cold as any stone.'

[G. Account of the Life and Writings of Shakespeare.]

It is an incredible tale. Falstaff to die, to be cold, to call mournfully upon his God ... it is pitiful, and as he died he played with flowers, those things nearest to his beloved earth. For he loved the earth; he had the traits of the peasant, his lusts, his simplicity, his coarseness and his unquestioning faith. His guide was a rough and jovial Epicureanism, which rated equally with pleasure the avoidance of pain; Falstaff loved pleasure but was too simple to realise that pleasure must be paid for; the giant wanted or the giant did not want, and there was an end of the matter. He viewed life so plainly that he was ready to juggle with words and facts, so as to fit it to his desires; thus, when honour offended him, he came to believe there was no honour, to refuse God the death he owed him because of honour: 'Yea, but how if honour prick me off when I come on? how then? Can honour set a leg? No. Or an arm? No. Or take away the grief of a wound? No. Honour hath no skill in surgery then? No. Who hath it? he that died o' Wednesday. Doth he feel it? No. Doth he hear it? No. It is insensible then? Yea, to the dead. But will it not live with the living? No. Why? Detraction will not suffer it. Therefore I'll none of it; honour is a mere scutcheon; and so ends my catechism.'

Casuist! But he was big enough to deceive himself. Such casuistry was natural to the Englishman of Falstaff's day, who took his Catholicism as literally as any Sicilian peasant may take his to-day. Of Falstaff's unquestioning faith there is no doubt at all; his familiar modes of address of the Deity, his appeal when dying, his probable capacity for robbing a friar and demanding of him absolution, all these are indications of a simplicity so great that casuistry alone could rescue him from the perilous conclusions drawn from his faith. This is a difficulty, for Falstaff is not entirely the Englishman of to-day; he is largely the boisterous, Latinised Englishman of the pre-Reformation period; he is almost the typical Roman Catholic, who preserved through his sinful life a consciousness that faith would save him. But the human sides of Falstaff are wholly English; his love of meat and drink, his sleepiness, his gout, his coarseness (which was free from depravity), all these live to-day in the average Englishman of the well-to-do-classes, that Englishman who dislikes the motor-car but keeps a hunter he is too fat to ride, who prefers suet pudding to any hotel bavaroise, and who, despite his gout (inherited from Falstaff), is still a judge of port.

That Englishman is not quite Falstaff, for he has lost his gaiety; he does not dance round the maypole of Merrie England; he is oppressed by cares and expenditures, he fears democracy and no longer respects aristocracy: the old banqueting-hall in which Falstaff rioted is tumbling about his ears. Yet he contains the Falstaffian elements and preciously preserves them. He is no poet, but he still enshrines within him, to burst out from among his sons, the rich lyrical verse which, Mr Chesterton truly says, belongs primarily to the English race. The poetry which runs through Falstaff is still within us, and his philosophy radiates from our midst. The broad tolerances of England, her taste for liberty and ease, her occasional bluster and her boundless conceit, all these are Falstaffian traits and would be eternal if admixture of Celtic blood did not slowly modify them. Falstaff contains all that is gross in England and much that is fine; his cowardice, his craft, his capacity for flattery are qualifying factors, for they are not English, any more than they are Chinese: they are human, common. But the outer Falstaff is English, and the lawless root of him is yet more English, for there is not a race in the world hates the law more than the English race. Thus the inner, adventurous Falstaff is the Englishman who conquered every sea and planted his flag among the savages; he is perhaps the Englishman who went out to those savages with the Bible in his hand; he is the unsteady boy who ran away to sea, the privateersman who fought the French and the Dutch; he is the cheerful, greedy, dull, and obstinate Englishman, who is so wonderfully stupid and so wonderfully full of common sense. Falstaff was never crushed by adversity: no more was the English race; it was, like him, too vain and too optimistic, too materially bounded by its immediate desires. It is not, therefore, wild to claim him as the gigantic ancestor and kindly inspiration of the priests, merchants, and soldiers who have conquered and held fields where never floated the lilies of the French or the castles of the Portuguese. Too dull to be beaten and too big to be moved, Falstaff was the Englishman.

3. MÜNCHAUSEN

Exaggeration is a subtle weapon and it must be handled subtly. Handled without skill it is a boomerang, recoils upon the one who uses it and makes of him a common liar; under the sway of a master it is a long bow with which splendid shafts may be driven into human conceit and human folly. There have been many exaggerators in history and fiction since the days of Sindbad, and they have not all been successful; some were too small, dared not stake their reputation upon a large lie; some were too serious and did not know how to wink at humanity, put it in good temper and thus earn its tolerance; and some did not believe their own stories, which was fatal.

For it is one thing to exaggerate and another to exaggerate enough. A lie must be writ so large as to become invisible; it must stand as the name of a country upon a map, so much larger than its surroundings as to escape detection. One may almost in the cause of invention, parallel the saying of Machiavelli, 'If you make war, spare not your enemy,' and say 'If you lie, let it not be by halves'; let the lie be terrific, incredible, for it will then cause local anæsthesia of the brain, compel unreasoning acceptance in the stunned victim. If the exaggerator shrinks from this course his lie will not pass; it might have passed, and I venture a paradox, if it had been gigantic enough. The gigantic quality in lies needs definition; evidently the little 'white' lie is beyond count, while the lie with a view to a profit, the self-protective lie, the patriotic lie and the hysterical, vicious lie follow it into obscurity. One lie alone remains, the splendid, purposeless lie, born of the joy of life. That is the lie of braggadocio, a shouting, rich thing, the mischievous, arch thing beloved of Münchausen. The Baron hardly lied to impress his friends; he lied to amuse them and amuse himself. To him a lie was a hurrah and a loud, resonant hurrah, because it was big enough.

In the bigness of the lie is the gigantic quality of the liar. If, for instance, we assume that no athlete has ever leapt higher than seven feet, it is a lie to say that one has leapt eight. But it is not a gigantic lie: it is a mean, stupid lie. The giant must not stoop so low; he must leap, not eight feet, but eight score, eight hundred. He must leap from nebula to nebula. If he does not claim to have achieved the incredible he is incredible in the gigantic sense. Likewise he is not comic unless he can shock our imagination by his very enormity. We do not laugh at the pigmy who claims an eight-foot leap; we sneer. Humour has many roots, and exaggeration is one of them, for it embodies the essential incongruous; thus we need the incongruity of contrast between the little strutting man and the enormous feat he claims to have achieved.

If Münchausen is comic it is because he is not afraid; his godfather, the Critical Review,[7] rightly claimed that 'the marvellous had never been carried to a more whimsical and ludicrous extent.' Because he was not afraid, we say 'Absurd person,' and laugh, not at but with him. We must laugh at the mental picture of the Lithuanian horse who so bravely carried his master while he fought the Turk outside Oczakow, only to be cut in two by the portcullis ... and then greedily drank at a fountain, drank and drank until the fountain nearly ran dry because the water spouted from his severed (but still indomitable) trunk! The impossible is the comedy of Münchausen; when he approaches the possible his mantle seems to fall from him. For instance, in a contest with a bear, or rather one of the contests, for Münchausen seemed to encounter bears wherever he went, he throws a bladder of spirits into the brute's face, so that, blinded by the liquor, it rushes away and falls over a precipice. This is a blemish; a mortal hunter might thus have saved himself with his whisky-flask; this is not worthy of Münchausen. For Münchausen, to be comic, must do what we cannot do, thrust his hand into the jaws of a wolf, push on, seize him by the tail and turn him inside out. Then he can leave us with this vision before our eyes of the writhing animal nimbly treated as an old glove.

[7: December, 1785.]

In such scenes as these contests with bears, wolves, lions, crocodiles, the Baron is the chief actor, plays the part of comedian, but he is big enough to shed round himself a zone of comic light. The giant makes comedy as he walks; notably in St Petersburg, he runs from a mad dog, discarding his fur coat in his hurry, and that, so far as he is concerned, is the end of the adventure. But a comic fate pursues Münchausen, for his fur coat, bitten by the mad dog, develops hydrophobia, leaps at and destroys companion clothing, until its master arrives in time to see it 'falling upon a fine full-dress suit which he shook and tossed in an unmerciful manner.' That is an example of the comic zone in which Münchausen revolves; round him the inanimate breathes, is animated by his own life-lust until the 'it' of things vanishes into the magic 'he.'

It is a pity, from the purely comic point of view, that the Baron should so uniformly dominate circumstances. A victorious hero is seldom so mirth-making as is the ridiculous and ridiculed Tartarin; we find relief when Münchausen fails to throw a piece of ordnance across the Dardanelles, and when he shatters his chariot against the rock he thus decapitates and makes into Table Mountain. His failure, injurious to his gigantic quality, is essential to his comic quality, for the reader often cries out, in presence of his flaming victories: Accursed sun! Will you never set? But the sun of Münchausen will never set. For a moment it may be obscured by a passing cloud, while its powerful rays rebelliously glow through the clot of mist and maintain the outline of the Baron's wicked little eye, but set it cannot: is it not in its master's power to juggle with moons and arrest the steeds of Apollo?

Demigodly, the giant must see but not judge, for one cannot judge when one is so far away. Thus Münchausen has but few sneers for little mankind; he observes that the people of an island choose as governors a man and his wife who were 'plucking cucumbers on a tree' because they fell from the tree on the tyrant of the isle and destroyed him, but he does not seem to see anything singular in this method of government. Nor has he an express scoff for the College of Physicians because no deaths happened on earth while it was suspended in the air. The scoff is there, but it is not expressed by Münchausen; he takes the earth in his hand, remarks 'Odd machine, this,' and lays it down again. And it may be too much to say 'odd'; though Münchausen expresses astonishment from time to time it is not vacuous astonishment; it is reasonable, measured astonishment, that of a modern tourist in Baedekerland. Thus, in his view, politicians, rulers, pedagogues, apothecaries, explorers are not subjects for his sling: they are curiosities.

He stares at these curiosities with simple wonder. He does not see the world as a joke, but as an earnest and extraordinary thing. He is always ready to be mildly surprised and he is never sceptical; that is, he never doubts the possibility of the impossible when it happens to him: he gravely doubts it when it happens to anybody else. Thus it is clear that he does not think much of Mr Lemuel Gulliver, that his chief enemy is his old rival Baron de Tott. If he were not so polite Münchausen would call de Tott a plain liar; he refrains and merely outstrips the upstart, as a gentleman should do. Münchausen sees the world in terms of himself; he would have no faith in the marvellous escapes of von Trenck, Jack Sheppard, and Monte Cristo. 'I,' says Münchausen, and the rivals may withdraw. He does not even fear imitation, and if he were confronted with Dickens's story of the lunars in Household Words, or with his French imitator, M. de Crac, he would chivalrously say: 'Most creditable, but I....' Nothing in Münchausen is so colossal as his 'I.' Like the Gauls he fears naught, save that the sky will fall upon his head, and I am not sure that he fears even that: the accident might enable him to make interesting notes on heaven.

There is, perhaps, unjustified levity in this surmise of mine, for Münchausen is a pious man. When, in Russia, he covers an old man with his cloak, a voice from heaven calls to him: 'You will be rewarded, my son, for this in time.' It must have been the voice of St Hubert, the patron to whom Münchausen readily paid his homage, for Münchausen simply believed in him, liked to think that 'some passionate holy sportsman, or sporting abbot or bishop, may have shot, planted, and fixed the cross between the antlers of St Hubert's stag.' But his piety is personal; he believes that the voice is for him alone, that St Hubert is his own saint. Gigantic Münchausen shuts out his own view of the world. His shadow falls upon and obscures it. That is why he so continuously brags. The most resolute horseman shrinks from a wild young horse, but Münchausen tames him in half an hour and makes him dance on the tea-table without breaking a single cup; the Grand Seignior discards his own envoy and employs him on State business at Cairo; he makes a cannon off a cannon-ball, 'having long studied the art of gunnery'; he does away (in his third edition) with the French persecutors of Marie Antoinette. He, always he, is the actor; he is not the chief actor, he is the sole actor, and the rest of the world is the audience.

So simply and singly does he believe in himself that his gigantic quality is assured. He disdains to imitate; when confined in the belly of the great fish he does not wait like Sindbad, or wait and pray like Jonah: Baron Münchausen dances a hornpipe. He is quite sure that he will escape from the fish: the fish is large, but not large enough to contain the spirit of a Münchausen; and he is sure that the story is true. There is nothing in any adventure to show that the Baron doubted its accuracy, and we must not conclude from his threat in Chapter VIII.: 'If any gentleman will say he doubts the truth of this story, I will fine him a gallon of brandy and make him drink it at one draught,' that he knew himself for a liar. As a man of the world he recognised that his were wonderful stories, and he expected to encounter unbelief, but he did not encounter it within himself. No, Münchausen accepted his own enormity, gravely believed that he 'made it a rule always to speak within compass.' If he winked at the world as he told his tales it was not because he did not believe in them; he winked because he was gay and, mischievously enough, liked to keep the world on the tenterhooks of scepticism and gullibility. He did not even truckle to his audience, try to be in any way consistent; thus, when entangled with the eagle he rides in the branches of a tree, he dares not jump for fear of being killed ... while he has previously fallen with impunity some five miles, on his descent from the moon, with such violence as to dig a hole nine fathoms deep.

No, this precursor of Bill Adams, who saved Gibraltar for General Elliott, simply believed. Like Falstaff, like Tartarin, he suffered from mirage; though some of his adventures are dreams, monstrous pictures of facts so small that we cannot imagine them, others are but the distortions of absolutely historic affairs. No doubt Münchausen saw a lion fight a crocodile: it needed no gigantic flight for him to believe that he cut off the lion's head while it was still alive, if he actually cut it off 'to make sure' when it was dead; and though he did not tie his horse to a snow-surrounded steeple, he may have tied him to a post and found, in the morning, that the snow had so thawed as to leave the horse on a taut bridle; assuredly he did not kill seventy-three brace of wildfowl with one shot, but the killing of two brace was a feat noble enough to be magnified into the slaughter of a flight.

Münchausen lied, but he lied honestly, that is to himself before all men. For he was a gentleman, a gentleman of high lineage the like of whom rode and drove in numbers along the eighteenth century roads. His own career, or rather that of his historian, Raspe,[8] harmonises with his personal characteristics, reveals his Teutonic origin, and it matters little whether he was the German

'Münchausen' or the Dutch Westphalian 'Munnikhouson.' The first sentence of his first chapter tells of his beard; his family pride stares us everywhere in the face; Münchausen claims descent from the wife of Uriah (and he might have been innocent enough to accept Ananias as a forbear), and knows that noblesse oblige, for, says he to the Lady Fragantia when receiving from her a plume: 'I swear ... that no savage, tyrant, or enemy upon the face of the earth shall despoil me of this favour, while one drop of the blood of the Münchausens doth circulate in my veins!' Quixotic Münchausen, it is well that you should, in later adventures, meet and somewhat humiliate the Spanish Don. For you are a gentleman of no English and cold-blooded pattern, even though you buy your field-glasses at Dollonds's and doubtless your clothes at the top of St James's Street. Too free, too unrestrained to be English you maintain an air of fashion, you worship at the shrine of any Dulcinea.

[8: See Mr Thomas Seccombe's brilliant introduction to the Lawrence and Bullen edition, 1895.]

Münchausen has no use for women, save as objects for worship; they must not serve, or co-operate; for him they are inspiration, beautiful things before whom he bows, whom he compliments in fulsome wise; he is preoccupied by woman whenever he is not in the field; he has chivalrous oaths for others than the Lady Fragantia; he makes the horse mount the tea-table for the ladies' pleasure; he receives gracefully the proposals of Catherine of Russia; he is the favourite of the Grand Seignior's favourite; he is haunted by the Lady Fragantia, who was 'like a summer's morning, all blushing and full of dew.'

Polite and gallant as any cavalier, Münchausen carries in him the soul of a professor; he is minute, he kills no two score beasts, but exactly forty-one; every little thing counts for him, as if he were a student: Montgolfier and his balloon, architecture, and the amazing etymology for which 'Vide Otrckocsus de Orig-Hung.' A swordsman and a scholar he recalls those reiters who fled from kings into monasteries, there to labour as Benedictines. And he has Teutonic appetites. Indeed nothing is so Germanic as the Baron's perpetual concern with food: he remembers how good was the cherry-sauce made from the cherries that grew out of the stag's forehead; he gloats over a continent of cheese and a sea of wine; even on eagleback he finds bladders of gin and good roast-beef-fruit; bread-fruit, plum-pudding-fruit (hot), Cape wine, Candian sugar, fricassee of pistols, pistol-bullets, gunpowder sauce, all these figure in his memoirs. And if, sometimes, he is a little gross, as when he stops a leak in a ship by sitting upon it, which he can do because he is of Dutch extraction, he confirms completely the impression we have of him: a gallant gentleman, brave in the field, lusty at the trencher, gay in the boudoir.

Good Münchausen, you strut large about the Kingdom of Loggerheads, debonair, tolerant, confident; you believe in yourself, because so large that you cannot overlook yourself; you believe in yourself because you tower and thus amaze humanity; and you believe in yourself because you are as enormously credulous as you would have us be. Thus, because you believe in yourself, you are: you need no Berkeley to demonstrate you.

The Esperanto of Art

It is established and accepted to-day that a painter may not like music, that a writer may yawn in a picture-gallery: though we proclaim that art is universal, it certainly is not universal for the universe. This should not surprise us who know that van Gogh wrote: 'To paint and to love women is incompatible'; van Gogh was right for himself, which does not mean that he was right for everybody, and I will not draw from his dictum the probably incorrect conclusion that 'To paint and to love literature is incompatible.' But van Gogh, who had not read Bergson, was indicating clearly enough that he knew he must canalise his powers, therefore exclude from his emotional purview all things which did not appertain directly to his own form of art.

Form of art! Those three words hold the difficulty of mutual understanding among artists. While sympathising with van Gogh in his xenophobia, I cannot accept that because certain artists did not appreciate certain forms of art, no artist can understand another whose form is alien to him. There is, there must be a link between the painter, the sculptor, the writer, the musician, the actor, between the poet in words and the one, to-day most common, who wishes to express himself in the deeds of his own life. For art is, we are assured thereof, all of one stuff. A symphony and a poem may be allotropic forms of the same matter: to use a common simile, there is red phosphorus and there is yellow, but both are phosphorus. Likewise there are different forms of art, but there is only one art.

It is important that artists should understand one another so that conflict may arise from their impressions, so that they may form a critical brotherhood. Some, to-day, are able to grasp one another's meaning and yet find it difficult, because every form of art has its own jargon, to express what they mean; they can grasp that the painter equally with the writer is striving to express himself, but they fail to phrase their appreciation and their criticism because writers cannot talk of masses or painters of style. There stands between them a hedge of technique; so thick is it that often they cannot see the spirit of the works; their difficulty is one of terms. Now I do not suggest that the musician should study Praxiteles and himself carve marble; he is better employed expressing his own passion in the Key of C. But I do feel that if technical terms are the preserve of each form of art, general terms are not; that continuity, rhythm, harmony, to quote but a few, have a precise meaning, that they are inherent in no form of art because they are inherent in art itself.

The following, then, is a forlorn attempt to find the common language, the esperanto of art. It is made up of general terms (in italics); it represents no more than a personal point of view, and is for this reason laid down in a tentative spirit: it is not a solution but a finger-post. Order being a necessary antidote for the abstruse, I have divided the terms into groups, according to their nature, to the dimension they affect or the matter to which they refer. Following this line of thought we find that works of art affect us in virtue of four properties: their power, their logic, their movement, and their attitude; this leads us to four groups of properties:—

Group A. (Volumetric): Concentration, Relief, Density, Depth.

Group B. (Linear): Linking Continuity.

Group C. (Kinetic): Rhythm, Intensity, Reaction, Key, Culmination.

Group D. (Static): Grace, Balance, Harmony.

This is a rough classification, for an opera does not necessarily compare with a square rood of paint or a novel of Tolstoyan length; indeed, on the volumetric basis, an opera may have less bulk than a sonnet.

Group A. (Volumetric). By concentration we mean the quality of conveying a great deal within a small space. It follows that concentration is in inverse ratio to area, though it does not follow that area is in inverse ratio to concentration. While Anna Karenin is an enormous novel it is as concentrated as the sonnet of d'Arvers; on the other hand, Francis Thompson's Arab Love Song is more concentrated than the complete works of Mrs Barclay; while any Rubens is more concentrated than a modern miniature, an intaglio may be more concentrated than twenty square yards of Delacroix. We nullify areas, therefore, and must lay down that the test of concentration is the effect: if the painter realises that the author has felt all he wrote, if the writer sees that every line was necessary, then both can be sure that they are respectively in presence of concentrated works.

Likewise with relief. A bas-relief may have none. A fresco may. Relief then is a matter of contrast, as is shown especially in the mosaics of Taj Mahal; but its nature is easily seen if we compare prose with paint:—

'He stood at the edge of the sea while the waves crept towards him, nearer and nearer, sinuously flowing and ebbing, but ever nearer. Ever.'

I give this as an instance, not as a fragment of literature. The lonely 'ever' gives relief to the sentence of twenty-four words if we assume that another long sentence follows. (If no sentence follows, 'ever' is no longer relief but culmination, see Group C.) The painter renders the same effect by a more vivid line of foam in the middle distance, the musician by interposing a treble motif between basses. Thus, if we find variety of sentence, variety of tone, we have relief.

Density and Depth need not detain us long. Flaubert, the Psalms, Jacob Epstein's Oscar Wilde, the Eroica and Velasquez all give the sensation we call by those names; we mean by them that the work contains a suggestion of something behind. Atmospheric quality, then, together with thought withdrawn, echo unheard and space unlimned, are the bases on which the two terms rest. The suggestion that this 'behind' exists is of course essential, for we must not conclude that where there is nothing to be seen there is something to be guessed: there must be no guessing, but if a feeling of reserve is created then density and depth exist.

Group B. (Linear). The quality of linking is opposed to the quality of discord, though a discord may prove to be a link. The most perfect instances of linking and continuity, for I almost identify the terms, are the solar spectrum and the song of the lark, but in the field of art we must be content with the gamut, the sequence of shades and the concatenation of phrases. In prose:—

'The bird rose up into the air, and its wings beat slowly. The air was laden with mist. The bird rose towards the clouds ...' is an instance where there is a solution of continuity, which could be remedied if the second sentence were related to the flight of the bird. And the same lack of continuity would exist if the painter of a harlequin were to make his skull-cap brown, if in a pause of some work of Locatelli the musician interposed (however skilfully and gradually) some characteristic Grieg chords.

It does not, of course, follow that a discord is discontinuous. Providing it recurs within the scheme of the work, as the clashes in Elektra, the sequence of discords becomes a sequence of links, and we arrive at this paradox, that it is the solutions of continuity provide the continuity, while the apparently continuous portions of the work are carried by the discordant sections. Thus there is continuity in the Louvre Ghirlandajo because equivalent, if minor, discords repeat the motif of the red mantle in two other portions of the picture. The relation of the discords is sometimes vital to more than continuity, namely to rhythm (Group C.).

With Group C. (Kinetic) we touch the most vital portion of the subject, for the kinetic quality in art amounts to the quality of life in man. And its chief component is rhythm. If rhythm be taken as a condition of internal movement within the inanimate, as a suggestion of expanding and retracting life, of phrases (musical, pictorial, or literary) that come to an inevitable resolution, it is seen that its presence in a work of art must baffle until it is realised under what guise it appears. A simple instance of prose rhythm is:—

'The wayfarer stopped by the well. He looked within its depths and the water was far below. Idly he dropped a pebble between the walls; and it seemed minutes while he waited until the water sped its thanks.'

This is not metrical but rhythmic prose, and it would be wearisome if the rhythm were not altered from paragraph to paragraph; short sentences alternate with long at fixed intervals, or passive verbs are inset between actives, while Gothic words, juxtaposed to Latin, or adjectival combinations produce the same effect of rise and fall. The rhythm may be regular as the movement of a woman's breast or spasmodic within the regular as the flight of a gull.

Pictorially rhythm is best gauged by certain tapestries based on the flower backgrounds of Fergusson and Anne Estelle Rice. Assume a black square of cloth; if the flowers are grouped thus from left to right: dark red, pink, white, there is no rhythm, for the mental line is a mere downgrade; if they are grouped: dark red, light blue, dark green, there is no rhythm, for the mental line is a mere curve, a circular or perhaps parabolic basin; but if the grouping amounts to: dark red, pink, light blue, black, light green, cream, dark brown, there is a succession of ebb and flow, rise and fall, rhythm. And this applies to drawing also, if we accept that colour is indicated by line, that lines are colours and that colours are tenses. That line can indicate colour is beyond denial, for we accept that colour is not material while tone is material. Colour being the relation between an impression and the impression of colourlessness, and tone being the resultant translation of the intensity of the colour, then it is feasible to reproduce a red and blue combination by a green and yellow combination of equal contrast.[9] Therefore a combination of blacks may be made to balance a combination of even seven colours, provided the relative intensity (amount) of the blacks is in a true relation, in tone, with the relative intensity of the colours. C. R. W. Nevinson achieves this with grays and blacks, while Wyndham Lewis forgoes it.

[9: Hence, if the colour relations are maintained, it is correct to represent a blue-eyed rubicund man by red eyes and a violet face.]

The quality of rhythm being obvious in music needs no discussion; it is the only form of rhythm the popular can recognise, but if we accept the principles of grouping in phrase and colour, no musician will fail to recognise a sarabande in a dance of Matisse or in the posturings of Kellermann's clown.

As for intensity, with which goes reaction, for the first cannot exist without the second, it is naturally brought about by the rhythmic focusing of the subject's attention upon words, colours or notes. Intensity is marked, for instance, by the triplets of the Venusberg music, their continual slow billowing; it can be found, less easily, in phrases and colours, but it must exist if the work is art. In prose it is marked by a general nervousness of form and word:—

'Upon the crag the tower pointed to the sky like a finger of stone, and about its base were thick bushes, which had burst forth into flower patches of purple and scarlet. The air was heavy with their scent.'

Here the intensity is confined within the simile and the colour scheme; the intervening space corresponds to the background of a picture, while the final short sentence, purposely dulled, is the reaction. Evidently (and all the more so as I have chosen a pictorial effect) an analogous intensity could be obtained in a painting; the flower patches could be exaggerated in colour to the uttermost limit of the palette, while the reagent final sentence was figured by a filmy treatment of the atmosphere. The limit to intensity is the key in which the work is conceived. But the word key must not be taken in its purely musical sense; obviously, within the same piece the governing motif must not be andante at the beginning and presto at the end, but in artistic generalisations it must be taken as the spirit that informs rather than as the technical rule which controls. Thus, in literature, the key is the attitude of the writer: if in one part of the book his thought recalls Thackeray and in another Paul de Kock the key has been changed; and again if the left side of the picture is pointillist, the right side cubist, the key has been changed. I choose exaggerated, almost absurd instances to make the point clear; in practice, when the writer, the musician, or the painter appears to have seen consistently, the key he has worked in is steadfast.

It should be said that uniformity of key does not imply absence of reaction; there is room, while the key remains uniform, for the juxtaposition of burlesque and romance, just as there is room in Holbein's 'Ambassadors' for the incomprehensible object in the foreground, said to embody a pun (Hohl Bein). But the key needs to be kept in mind as its maximum expression is the culmination of the effect. The culmination of a speech is in its peroration; of a poem in its incorporated envoi. Thus in the Arab Love Song, the culmination is:—

'And thou what needest with thy tribe's black tents
Who hast the red pavilion of my heart?'

There is no difficulty there. But in painting the culmination is more subtle. It consists in the isolation of the chief object. Say that we have from left to right: Black, yellow, dark brown, light blue, dark red; then add on the extreme right, crimson, then gold. The picture culminates on the extreme right, with the result that attention is directed there and that any object in that section of the picture benefits by an influence about equivalent to that of footlights. Culmination, involves the painter in great difficulties, for there must be culmination, while an effect in the wrong place may destroy the balance of his work. This appertains to

Group D. (Static). Its chief quality, balance, is easily defined in painting. Where there is correspondence between every section of the picture, where no value is exaggerated, balance exists. Hence the failure of Futurism. While the Futurists understand very well intensity, reaction, and relief, they refuse to give balance any attention at all; leaving aside the absurdity of rendering the mental into terms of the pictorial, and taking as an instance one who was once less Futurist than the Futurists, Severini, we see in his 'Pan-pan Dance' how he detached himself from his school: he attained balance by giving every object an equal intensity. Such is also the tendency of Wadsworth. Evidently if there are no clashes of tone-values, there must be balance, and the instance serves to show that where there are clashes of tone-values balance must be ensured by the artist's hand. There is always balance in the purely decorative; in the realistic there is balance if the attention of the beholder is directed simultaneously to the several points of culmination indicated by the rhythm of the picture. Thus there is balance in Rothenstein's 'Chloe' because the rocks on the right repeat the significance of the rocks on the left.

Likewise in literature there is balance in certain groupings of phrases:—

'The waves rolled in. Every one, edged with foam, curved forward to kiss the sand. Silvery in the sun they rolled. And they came assured, as if they had forgotten that they had come at other dawns, only to retire before the inert earth.'

This is almost the exact 'short-long-short-long' of waves themselves, and there is balance because each short-long grouping figures one curled wave. Nothing clarifies this idea so well as the Morse Code.

With perfect balance go grace and harmony. While grace must stand by itself as a not especially important quality because it is not, need not, always be present, harmony must be recognised as a synonym of balance. It is only because grace is often used where harmony is meant that it finds a place in this glossary. Obviously there is no grace in Rodin's Balzac, while there is grace in every note of Lulli and Glück; by grace we mean the quality of lightness we find in Pater, Meredith, André Gide, Mozart, Watteau, Donatello: the instances suffice to indicate the meaning, while harmony, if it be taken as a synonym of balance, needs no further explanation than has been given for that term.

I venture to repeat in conclusion that there is nothing dogmatic about these ideas. They are subject to criticism and objection, for we are groping in the dark towards what Mr Leonard Inkster calls the standardisation of artistic terms; if I prefer to his scientific way the more inspired suggestion of 'esperanto,' that is a common language of the arts, it is without fear of being called metaphysical. It may be argued that a purely intellectual attempt to extract and correlate the inspirations of forms of art is a metaphysical exercise doomed to failure by its own ambition. I do not think so. For art is universal enough to contain all the appeals, the sensuous, the intellectual, and, for those who perceive it, the spiritual; but the sensuous is incapable of explanation because sensuousness is a thing of perceptions which vanish as soon as the brain attempts to state them in mental terms; and the spiritual, which I will define much as I would faith as a stimulation produced by a thing which one knows to be inexistent, also resists analysis; if we are to bridge the gulfs that separate the various forms of art, some intellectual process must be applied. Now it may be metaphysical to treat of the soul in terms of the intellect, but the intellect has never in philosophic matters refrained from laying hands upon the alleged soul of man; I see no reason, therefore, to place art higher than the essence of human life and grant it immunity from attack and exegesis by the intellect. Indeed, the intellect in its metaphysical moods is alone capable of solving the riddle of artistic sensation. Once defined by intellect and applied by intellect, the esperanto of the arts may well serve to reconcile them and demonstrate to their various forms, against their will, their fundamental unity.

The Twilight of Genius

I

Given that the attitude of the modern community towards genius is one of suspicion, modified by fear, I am inclined to wonder what a latter day Tarquinius would do in the garden of contemporary thought. The old Superb struck off the heads of those flowers grown higher than their fellows; he was ancestor to those who persecuted Galileo, Copernicus, Hargreaves, Papin, Manet, all the people who differed from their brethren and thus engendered the greatest malevolence of which man is capable: family hatred. I think Tarquinius has but himself to blame if there are to-day so few heads to strike off. He has struck off so many that in a spirit of self-protection genius has bred more sparingly. All allowances made for the hope from which the thought springs, I feel that we live on a soil watered by many tears, poor ground for genius to flourish in, where now and then it may sprout and wither into success, where glory is transmuted into popularity, where beauty is spellbound into smartness. My general impression is that genius is missing and unlikely of appearance; weakly, I turn to the past and say, 'Those were the days'; until I remember that in all times people spoke of the past and said 'Those were the days.' For the past is never vile, never ugly; it has the immense merit of being past. But even so, I feel that in certain periods, in certain places, genius could flourish better than it does in the midst of our underground railways and wireless telesynographs.

Our period is perhaps poor in genius because it is so rich in talent. There is so much talent that one can buy any amount of it for £400 a year, and a great deal more for two lines in an evening paper. Talent is the foe of genius; it is the offshoot from the big tree, which cannot itself become a tree, and yet weakens the parent stock. Indeed, it may be that the sunset of genius and the sunrise of democracy happened all within one day. In former times, so few men had access to learning that they formed a caste without jealousy, anxious to recruit from among ambitious youth. The opportunities of the common man were small; the opportunities of the uncommon man were immense. Perhaps because of this three of the richest epochs in mankind came about; the self-made merchant, writing to his son, was not wrong to say that there is plenty of room at the top, and no elevator; but he should have added that there was a mob on the stairs and on the top a press agency.

My general impression of the Medicis is a highly select society, centring round a Platonic academy which radiated the only available culture of the day, the Latin and the Greek. War, intrigue, clerical ambition, passion, and murder, all these made of a century a coloured background against which stand out any flowers that knew how to bloom. The small, parochial society of the Medicis wanted flowers; to-day, we want bouquets. It was the same in the big period that includes Elizabeth, the period that saw Sydney, Beaumont, Sir Walter Raleigh, Shakespeare, Spenser;—here again a nucleus of time haloed with the golden dust of thought, as a fat comet draws its golden trail. The Elizabethan period was the heroic time of English history, the time of romance, because it sought the unknown land and the unknown truth, because if some easily went from gutter to gallows, others as easily found their way from gutter to palace. This is true also of the period of Louis XIV., an inferior person, of barbarous vanity, of negligent uxoriousness, untiring stratagem, but a great man all the same because greedy of all that life can give, whether beautiful women, broad kingdoms, or sharp intellects. To please him, Molière, Boileau, Racine, and many of less importance, danced their little dance under the umbrella of his patronage. They are still dancing, and Louis XIV., that typical big-wig, stands acquitted.

When one thinks of these periods, one is, perhaps, too easily influenced, for one compares them with one's own, its haste, its scurry for money, its noisy hustle. One fails to see the flaws in other times, one forgets the spurns that merit of the unworthy took, the crumb that the poor man of thought picked up from the carpet of the man of place. But still, but still ... like an obstinate old lady, that is all one can say, one feels that those were better days for genius, because then respectability was unborn.

It may be that already my readers and I are at war, for here am I, glibly talking of genius, without precisely knowing what it is, as one may talk of art, or love, without being able to define those things; all one can do is to point out genius when one sees it. Carlyle was much laughed at for saying that genius was an infinite capacity for taking pains. That does not sound like genius; one imagines genius as ravelling its hair, whatever ravelling may be, and producing the immortal Word to the accompaniment of epileptic fits; absinthe also goes with genius very well. But in reality genius, I suspect, is a tamer affair, and arises easily enough in men like Rembrandt, who painted pictures because he liked doing it and because the sitters paid him for their portraits; more satisfactorily to Carlyle it arises in men like

Flaubert, who revealed much of his attitude in one phrase of his correspondence: 'To-day I have worked sixteen hours and have at last finished my page.' Therein lies the difference between Flaubert and de Maupassant; it may be, too, that Boileau was right in advising the poet a hundred times to replace his work upon the bench, endlessly polish it, and polish it again, but many instances of almost spontaneous creation confront us; it is enough to quote that in six years, between 1602 and 1608, Shakespeare appears to have written eleven plays, among them Julius Cæsar, Hamlet, Othello, Macbeth, and King Lear. What shall we say then of that vague thing, genius, which is to mankind what the thing some call soul is to man? For my part, I believe it to be volcanic rather than sedimentary. It is as if the spirit of the race had accumulated in a creature, the spirit of life claiming to be born. Genius will out, but it is most frequent in certain periods of human history, such as the Elizabethan or Medician, in certain places, such as France, Italy, and the Low Countries, under certain influences, such as oppression, war, revolution, or social decay. That is an interesting catalogue, and if history repeats itself, the future for genius, as evidenced particularly in art, would be black, for there has been no period where comfort, ease and security bred genius. It is as if the plant needed something to push against. Every day life becomes more secure, justice more certain, property more assured; humanity grows fat, and the grease of its comfort collects round its heart. It is difficult to imagine genius flourishing in a world perfectly administered by city councils.

It was not in worlds such as ours that the geniuses of the past sped their flights, but in anxious, tortured, corrupt, starving worlds, worlds of heaping ambition and often tottering fortune. Napoleon lived in one of those periods of reconstruction, when the earth bears new life, restores what the earth has just destroyed, a period very like this war (a hopeful sign, though I make no prophecies); but if Napoleon is remembered, it is not only as a conqueror, for other men have won battles and the dust of their fame is mingled with the dust of their bones. His genius does not lie in his military skill, in his capacity to pin a wing while piercing a centre, nor in his original idea that guns should be taken from battalions and massed into artillery brigades. The genius of Napoleon lies in the generality of his mind, in his understanding of the benefits the State would derive from the tobacco monopoly, in his conception of war as the victory of the transport officer, in his conception of peace as the triumph of law, which is the French Civil Code. It manifested itself when Napoleon in the middle of flaming Moscow, in a conquered country, surrounded by starving troops and massing enemies, could calmly peruse the law establishing the French state-endowed theatres and sign it upon a drumhead. That is typical, for genius is both general and particular. It is the quality to which nothing that is human can be alien, whether of mankind or of man. Lincoln was a man such as that; his passionate advocacy of the negro, his triumph at Cooper Union, his Gettysburg dedication, his administrative capacity, all that is little by the side of his one sentiment for the conquered South: 'I will treat them as if they had never been away.'

The detail, which is the prison house of the little man, is the exercising ground of the great one. Such men as Galileo showed what brand it was they would set upon history's face; the soul of Galileo is not in the telescope, or in the isochronism of the pendulum oscillation, or even in the discovery (which was rather an intuition) of the movement of the earth. All of Galileo is in one phrase, when poor, imprisoned, tortured and mocked, heretic and recusant, he was able to murmur to those who bade him recant: 'Still she moves.' It is in all of them, this general and this particular, in Leonardo, together painter, mathematician, architect, and excellent engineer, but above all father of La Gioconda. It is in Beethoven, not so much in the 'Pathétique' or in the 'Pastorale,' as in the man who, through his deafness, could still hear the songs of eternity. Special and general were they all; one comes to think that genius is together an infinite capacity for seeing all things, and an infinite capacity for ignoring all things but one.

Life goes marching on, who shall claim the laurel wreath that time cannot wither? So many, still living or recently dead, have postured so well that it is hard to say what will be left when they have been discounted at the Bank of Posterity. Politicians, writers, men of science, highly prized by their fellows ... what living court is cool enough to judge them? Who shall say whether Rodin will remain upon a pedestal, or whether he will fall to a rank as low as that of Lord Leighton? Likewise, Dr Ehrlich saw the furrow he ploughed crossed by other furrows; it may be that the turbulent, inquisitive mind of Mr Edison may have developed only fascinating applications, and not have, as we think, set new frontiers to the field of scientific thought. Those are men difficult to fix, as are also men such as Lord Kitchener and Henry James, because they are too close to us as persons to be seen entirely, and yet too far for us to imagine the diagrams of their personalities. We are closer to some others, to people such as Mr Thomas Hardy, even though he stopped in full flight and gathered himself together only to produce the Dynasts in a medium which is not quite the one he was born to. We are fairly close, too, to Mr Anatole France, to his gaiety, his malignancy, his penetration without excessive pity. Mr Anatole France is one of the great doubtfuls of our period, like the Kaiser and Mr Roosevelt. Like both, he has something of the colossal, and like both he suggests that there were, or may be, taller giants. For as one reads Mr Anatole France, as he leads one by the hand through Ausonian glades, the shadow of Voltaire haunts one wearing a smile secure and vinegary. Likewise, when we consider the Kaiser, where depth has been transmuted into area, where responsibility to his own pride borders upon mania, appraisal is difficult. The Kaiser, judging him from his speeches and his deeds, appears to have carried the commonplace to a pitch where it attains distinction. He has become as general as an encyclopædia; he is able to embrace in a single brain theocracy and local government, official art and zoology; he has carried respect for the family to the limit of patriarchal barbarity ... one loses all sense of proportion and ceases to know whether he is colossal or monstrous. In many ways one discovers brotherhood in people like Cecil Rhodes, the Kaiser, and Mr Roosevelt. All three are warriors in a modern Ring, and all three suggest displacement from their proper period, for I imagine the Kaiser better as a Frederick Barbarossa, Cecil Rhodes as an all-powerful Warren Hastings, and Mr Roosevelt as a roaring Elizabethan sailor, born to discover and ravage some new kind of Spanish Main.

They are not easily passed through the gauge of criticism, these people. Their angles have not worn off, so that many doubtfuls, such as Carlyle, Whitman, de Maupassant, Beaconsfield, people who dumped themselves in history and stayed there, because one did not know how to move them, put their names down as candidates to the immortal roll. Excepting perhaps Mr Anatole France, it is difficult to tell where they will pass eternity. If we cannot say who of our fathers may claim the laurel wreath, how can we choose from among ourselves? We judge our fathers so harshly that it is a comfort to think we may be as unjust to our sons ... but what of ourselves? of this generation which feels so important that it hardly conceives a world without itself? a generation like other generations in the Age of Bronze, that felt so advanced because the Age of Stone had gone by? Let us name nobody, and consider rather the times in which we sow our seeds.

They are not very good times, these modern ones. Historically speaking, they are not the sort of times which favour genius; though it be true that genius is volcanic, there are conditions which assist its birth, which give tongues to inglorious Miltons. It is so, just as certain times and conditions can stifle even genius, and the paradox is that both are the same. Poverty can kill genius, and it can make it; oppression may clip its wings or grow its feathers; disease may sap its strength, or flog its nerves. Epictetus was a slave. But one feature of our period is its devouring hatred of anything worthy of being called art; thus have come about two decays, that of the artist and that of art. A vivid and vulgarised world has deprived us of an aloof audience, for the aristocrats who once were cultured are photographed in the papers. Haste, crudity, sensation, freedom from moral, religious, social ties have brought about a neglect of fine shades. Thus, when I consider the conditions created in every civilised State by the present war, when speech is repressed, where letters are read, rebels banished, where the songs of the muses are drowned by the yapping of the popular curs, I find hope in humanity, because it is a sleepy thing and often asserts its greatness when it is most reviled. To take a minor instance (and let us not exaggerate its value), I doubt if post-impressionists, futurists, cubists, and such like would have achieved the little they have, if they had not felt outcast, a sort of gray company marching into the lonely dawn. Oh yes! some of them (but not all) are small people, absurd people, many of them; they will be followed by other people quite as small and as petty, and they will set to work to astonish the bourgeois. At that game, one of them may manage to stagger humanity.

I suspect that three main qualities affect the occurrence of genius: the emotional quality of a period, its intellectual and its romantic quality. It is not easy to discern those three qualities in the modern world, because of the growing uniformity of mankind. The individual is greater than the citizen, and yet a deep-dyed national livery brings him out. As civilisation spreads, in all white countries other than Russia it tends to produce a uniform type; at any rate, it produces uniform groups of types. For instance, if we measure types by their anxiety to gain money or status, by the houses in which they agree to live, by the clothes they wear, the foods and the pleasures they like, we find little difference between the industrial, districts of Lombardy and Sheffield, the coal mines and factories of Lille, or those of Pennsylvania. Likewise, if we compare elegance, hurry, display, intellectual keenness, a man will find all he wants, whether he live in Paris, in Vienna, in New York, or in London. (I have eaten dinner at the Metropole, London, the Metropole, Paris, the Metropole, Brussels, and the Continental, San Sebastian; and it was the same dinner everywhere, more or less: Suprème de Volaille, Riz à l'Impératrice, etc.). Even the farmers, those laggards, have lost so many of their ancient ways that from Sussex to Kentucky identities have sprung up. The races, now that railways and steamers have come, mingle freely, exchange dishes, plays, and entangle themselves matrimonially in foreign lands. It was less so in 1850, and it was hardly so in 1800. Following on travel, and on the growth of foreign trade, the study of foreign languages has sprung up, so that most of us are fit to become ambassadors or waiters. Education, too, which in its golden age taught no man anything that would be of the slightest practical use to him, that contented itself with making him into a man of culture, has in all white countries set itself the task of fitting men, by the means of languages, cheap science, geography and book-keeping, to force life to pay dividends. Only life pays no dividends; it merely increases its capital.

This similarity of life, induced by the modern applications of science, the railway, the telegraph, the telephone, double-entry, the steamer, the film, has denationalised man, and however many wars he may wage in the cause of nationality, he will continue to grow denationalised, because the contact of neighbours, which he cannot avoid, teaches him to desire what they enjoy; he can attain his desire only by becoming more like them. I doubt if this is the best atmosphere for the rise of genius.

Retirement within self, followed by violent emergence, one of the conditions of genius, is more easily attained in an enclosed community of the type of ancient Florence than in a sort of international congress like Chicago. The sensation of being a chosen people, felt by all strong nationalities, such as the Elizabethan English, the 'Mayflower' settlers, the Jews, the Castilians, provides the stimulus to pride, which spurs into the gallop of genius a talent which might trot. Thus the Chinese potters, and the Japanese painters of the past, produced their unequalled work ... while of late years they have taken to European ways, and have come to paint so ill that they are admired in respectable drawing rooms.

Molière was a Frenchman; his humour is not that of Falstaff, nor of Aristophanes, nor of Gogol. He was a Frenchman first, and a genius after. Likewise, Cervantes was a Spaniard, and Turgenev a Russian. None of them could be anything else. But they did not carry their nation: they rode it; though genius express the world, its consciousness of its own people expresses that people. The nationality of a man of genius is a sort of tuning fork which tells him all the time whether his word or his deed is ringing true to his own being.

It is not wonderful that in such conditions the emotional quality of our time should be hard to discern, for it is not easy to survey a boiling world. That quality can be expressed only through four media—art, patriotism, religion, and love. Art, which, of course, includes letters, is not in a very good state. There is the one sculptor, Jacob Epstein, who detaches himself and makes a bid for a pedestal; Mestrovic, his Serbian rival, tends to the colossal rather than to the great. In painting, the chaos is perhaps pregnant, but it is still chaos; not one of our young cubists or futurists can pretend to be anything more than a finger-post. In literature, Italy, Germany, and Austria are desert, while France, represented by men such as Mr Paul Fort, the late Marcel Proust, the much boomed Mr Barbusse, and Mr Claudel, seems to have reached the nadir of decay. If the writers of the day were not mortal and the future leisurely, the Germans (though they have nothing to boast of) might well argue that France should take her farewell benefit. England is happier, even though nearly all her young novelists are afflicted with a monstrous interest in themselves, and an equally monstrous lack of sympathy with everybody else. They are in reaction against surrounding life, builders and destroyers as well as showmen. Their seniors, who once bid so high, such as Mr Bennett and Mr Wells, have taken the fatal plunge which leads to popularity, but the younger ones have produced one man, Mr D. H. Lawrence, prejudiced, diseased in outlook, hectic and wandering, who has the exquisite feeling for natural beauty, the rhapsodic quality which may make of him a prose Shelley, if not a prose neurotic. America does not come in yet; she is too old to bring forth the genius of the pioneer, too young to bring forth the genius of maturity. The time of the Hawthornes has gone, and the time of the Dreisers is not yet. It is true, though likely to be disputed, that in men such as Mr Theodore Dreiser and Mr Owen Johnson, men who write badly and vulgarly, whose works are either sentimental or brutish, America must look to her claimants for literary fame. Those men are alive; they will fail like Jack London, but they indicate the trend of America and represent the violent quality of her fresh-painted civilisation. Other men, in other times, will sing their songs; to a country like America, what is five hundred years?

The emotional quality of our time is no better expressed in patriotism, however prevalent this emotion may be just now. The patriotism which to-day reigns in the world is rather a negative thing; it consists much more in hating enemies than in loving friends. It is a smoky, dusty, bloody, angry affair. It calls up every heroism and every ugliness. There is so much drama in the world that our sentiments grow dramatic, and we come to depend for our patriotic feelings upon the daily stimulus of newspapers, uniforms, and bands. All that is ephemeral because it lacks exaltation. The Germans enjoy a rather more romantic patriotism, because they are the most aggressive and the most guilty of what is happening ... and it is an irony that in this guilt should be found the ancient strength that made the unjust man flourish as the green bay tree. But their patriotism is, perhaps, the most shoddy, the most artificial of all: rhapsodies about the ancient German gods are ridiculous when we think that Germany is mainly a country of aniline factories; when they call a trench line the Siegfried Line (why not the Schopenhauer Redoubt?) they are ridiculous. Patriotism is not found in such theatrical eccentricities, any more than it is found in the constant courage of those who defend. Patriotism is in the brain, not in the body; it is love rather than hatred, a builder, not a destroyer. It opens its eyes towards fair horizons and plans cities in the clouds. It is an eternally young man who dreams dreams. Patriotism sailed with Columbus, held the hand of Necker and Witte, striving to reform their countries; it was in Grant rather than in the gallant Robert Lee. Patriotism so conceived does not haunt the streets, for it is a drab affair to give all one's energy to make the justice of one's country clean, to provide for its aged and its sick, to help it to grow learned or liberal. In peace times there are no patriots; there are only partisans.

We are told that emotion repressed finds its outlet in religion, but that is not true, for religion is now a decaying force, and every day rebellion grows against dogma. Let it be clear that ethics are not decaying, but these have nothing whatever to do with religion. In the true conception of religion many a rogue has gone to heaven, because by faith he gave it existence, while many a well-living churchwarden haunts another region, possibly because it was the only one that he could conceive. The modern world does not meditate on religion. It is interested in right and wrong, but it desires no extra-human solution of the problem of life, unless it can find it in the test-tube of a laboratory. It frankly does not care, and so the afflatus which swelled such triumphant men as St Augustine, Ignatius of Loyola, Torquemada, Mahomet, seeks sails to fill, but finds only steamboats. Religion, in its true meaning, an aspiration towards the divine, still exists among the Brahmins, but in a state of such quietism that it is sterile; it is lost to the whites. Differences of faith engender rivalry only, not hate, which is the next best thing to love. The doom of the faiths was written when their supporters lost the impulse to burn heretics.

Love is more fortunate, except that to-day too few bonds tie its wings, for it is the everlastingly real thing in the world. Mankind was charmed with its prowess in the age of stone, because it was the lyra upon which mortal man always thought to sing an immortal song. Love still sings its immortal songs, while the tramways go clanking by; it sings in daisy-spangled meadows and by the side of gasometers; its voice can dominate a nigger band, and there is no life it cannot embalm with the ashes of incense. But even so, many things soil it, the need for money in a civilisation where the gamble of life turns into an investment; there is social position, too, of which Henry VIII. thought very little, which means mainly that one always looks down upon somebody, always looks up to somebody, and seldom at anybody. But even so the satisfaction of love is too easy; if a man wishes to marry his cook, he has only to get rich and to give good dinners. (He would ... obviously.) He can be divorced and forgiven. No brutal duke can exile him or lock up his beloved in a convent. There are no Montagues and Capulets to duel in Piccadilly. A few banknotes and some audacity will buy the right to defy anything; barriers are coming down; classes are rising, others falling, and the time may not be far off when a Philadelphian maid will introduce her negro bridegroom.

III

Many factors go towards lowering the tone of this mankind whence genius should spring, as a madman or a god. One is our intense consciousness of money. The discovery of money is recent, for the rich men of the Bible wanted flocks and lands only so that they might eat well, drink well, and wed fair women; the lust of Ahab was rather unusual. At other times in Babylon, in Venice, wealth brought material benefits first, later only distinction. Only with the rise of the middle class did wealth become the greatest force, for it alone could make the middle class equal with their fellows. As they could claim no lineage, they naturally came to want to claim themselves better than their fellows; the merchant princes of the Victorian period, their sideboards, barouches, and sarcophagi, the American millionaires with their demon cars, their Ritz-Carlton dinners, their investments in old masters, (guaranteed mouldy), are natural consequences. Whereas in the seventeenth century you could impress if you were a duke, in the twentieth century if you become a millionaire you can stun. And you can stun only because everybody admires you for being a millionaire, because, as Miss Marion Ashworth perfectly says, 'there are people whom the mention of great fortunes always makes solemn.'

Even potential genius has been touched by this. Ruskin, Thackeray, Diaz, Kruger, all these loved money well, and all approached the state defined by Oscar Wilde: 'to know the price of everything and the value of nothing.' Love of money makes genius a laggard, for genius does not pay except in a run too long for most men's breath. 'Too long!' ... that is perhaps the cry of a century disinclined to take infinite pains.

With the demand for money goes the demand for fame. I doubt whether a genius still unrevealed will accept the idea that he may not achieve swift success. The fatal result is that potential genius is tempted to take the necessary steps to 'get-famous-quick'; that is to say, it must condescend. Instead of being one so high that none can understand him, the genius must become one just high enough to be admired. Then he is popular—and defeated, for as some Frenchman rightly said, he has earned the wages of popularity, which are the same as those of glory ... but paid out in coppers.

It is not altogether our fault, all this. The conditions in which we live do not favour the breeding of titans. Mr Dreiser's 'titan,' Cowperwood, his 'genius,' Witla, are fairly good instances of the modern view of genius. They are blatant, stupid, acquisitive, full of the vulgar strength which would have made of them successful saloon keepers. They cannot help it; they dwell in a world like an international exhibition, between a machine that can turn out seventeen thousand sausages an hour and the most expensive Velasquez on record; they thrive on the sweet draught of the soda fountain rather than on the honey of Hymettus, while the sun sees his horses unharnessed from his chariot and set to grinding out units of caloric power by the something or other company. This does not suit genius. Genius needs solitude, true solitude, not only a place where you cannot buy newspapers, but a place where there are none in the consciousness. Genius needs to retreat upon itself, to fecundate itself until from the nightmare of one life is born the dream of another. Genius cannot find this solitude, because the round globe hums as it spins, because it is alive with haste, with deeds crowding into the fleet hour that is no slower nor more rapid however crowded it may be, but only more hectic. We have come to a point where noise is natural, where we cannot sleep unless trains roar past our windows and newsboys cry murders to the unmoved night.

Literature has felt this of late years, and has retired into the country to find silence, but it is so nervous that silence stuns it. That will not last; many men of genius, Rembrandt, Whitman, Bach, Racine, felt this need to withdraw, even though most of them, in the country or in tiny towns, could well afford to mix with their fellows, because there were not enough of them to make a mob. They had their opportunity and could take it, and so they produced art which some thought to be an unhealthy secretion of the intellect. Their followers will not be so fortunate, and I have a growing vision of the world in the year 2500, when there may be but one State, one language, one race, when railways will have pushed their heads over the Himalaya at regular five-mile intervals, when there will be city councils on the shores of Lake Tanganyika, and Patagonia will stand first for technology. First? Perhaps not—it may be worse. I feel there may be no first, but a uniform level of mediocre excellence from which there will be no escape.

The intellectual prospects are better than the artistic, for the spirit of education overhangs the planet. It is true that education does not breed genius, but it breeds a type of man in whom arise intellectual manifestations akin to genius. Modern science has probably a large number of first principles to discover, and may have to destroy a good many principles now established; it will not need education for this, but it will need education to apply the new principles. A large mind can apprehend without special education, and it may be true that Isaac Newton traced the law of gravitation from the fall of an apple, that Mr Edison was led to the phonograph by a pricked finger, but it is much more true that the research man does not fluke upon the serum that will neutralise a disease germ, but will discover it by endless experiment and contrivance.

No educated man can discover a serum, or hope to design a multiphase dynamo. To do this astonishing work man needs a substratum of general and technical knowledge. This is being given him all over the world, where the classics are slowly vacating the schools and more quickly the universities, where elementary education is improving, where laboratory work is beginning to mean more than bangs and smells, where science applied to dyes, to foods, to metals, has established itself in a generation as a sort of elder sister to the pure science which came to us from alchemy. This goes further than science, which includes mathematics; not only are there thousands of schools for engineers, but the universities are developing on morphology, psychology, applied philosophy, history, law, constitutional practice, etc. This is happening all over the world and creating a sounder intellectual mind. That mind is far too specialised, but still it is a trained mind, a little more able than the old passionate mind to accept conclusions which do not square with its prejudices.

In France and Germany education is mainly utilitarian, which I think unfortunate, except from the point of view of intellectual production; in England, the desire for 'useful' education has not yet gone very far in the public schools, which still bring forth the admirable type of idiotic gentleman, but already in the old universities of Oxford and Cambridge there is a strong movement against compulsory Greek, which will develop against compulsory Latin. As the new universities in the manufacturing towns, Glasgow, Manchester, London, Leeds, Birmingham, grow up, the movement will be precipitated at Oxford and Cambridge, for they have always been kicked into leadership and no doubt will be kicked again. In America the movement is perhaps more pronounced, but more peculiar, because America appears to desire equally riches and culture. Certainly, Yale and Harvard no longer hold over other centres the hegemony which Oxford and Cambridge contrive to hold here. For America has not yet had time to make castes; she has been too busy making a great country.

I do not say that all this is agreeable. It is not, for education, once too deeply rooted in the useless, is throwing out equally dangerous roots into the useful. (As if we knew what is useful and what is useless in a life that must end in a passage through the needle's eye!) I do not like to think that a scholar should ask himself whether a subject will pay; it is distasteful that he should learn Russian to trade in Russia, and not to read Dostoievsky. There will be a reaction, for all fevers fall. A period must come when a new Virchow leads a crusade for the humanities, for philosophy, for the arts, and will make fashionable 'culture for culture's sake.' But before then the world must sink deeper into materialist education. That education will profit the world materially, because it makes the soil in which invention grows. It appears to be a good thing that ten ears of corn should be made to grow where once there grew but one, and so I suppose we must assume that it is a good thing if a machine can be induced to produce a million tin-tacks in ten minutes instead of half an hour, although I do not quite know why we should assume it. It is true that the boys and girls whom we draw from the poorer classes, whom we fill with dreams of becoming young gentlemen in black coats, and perfect ladies, are likely to produce a more nervous and intellectually acquisitive race, that they are more observant, more anxious to apprehend intellectually than were their forefathers, who only wanted to live. That class is to-day producing the industrial chemist, the technical agriculturalist, the electrician, the stone and timber expert, etc. The doctor, the solicitor, even the clergyman, are intellectually better trained than they were, more inclined to keep up-to-date by means of the journals of their societies and of the latest books. I think that class is likely to give us a sufficient group of Edisons, Pasteurs, Faradays, Röntgens. The coming centuries will inevitably see scientific developments which we only guess at: synthetic foods, synthetic fuels, metals drawn from the sea, the restoration of tissues, the prolongation of life, the applications of radio-active energy; we may assist at developments such as systematic thought transference, enlarge valuable organs such as the lungs, and procure the atrophy of useless ones such as the appendix. We have practically created protoplasm, and may soon reach the amoeba ... stumble perhaps a little further towards the triumph that would make man divine: the creation of life. We have everything to help us. Early genius was handicapped by having very little to build on, by finding it almost impossible to learn anything, because up to the eighteenth century anything and anybody intellectually valuable was burnt; early genius could depend only upon itself; it could not correlate its discoveries with those of others; nobody could assist it towards proof; genius always had to begin again at the beginning, and as a result made only occasional discoveries, so that the ignorance of the world was like an uncharted sea, dotted here and there with a ship of knowledge, unable to signal to another. That is over. No hypothesis is too daring, no claim is too great; every specialist is inflamed with an insatiable appetite for more knowledge, and on the whole he is willing to publish his own. This means that thousands, some of them men of talent, are co-operating on a single point, and it is quite possible that they will achieve more than the solitary outcast whom his fellows could not understand.

Such a future is not open to the arts, for they endeavour to-day to appeal not to small classes but to 'the public'; this means that they must startle or remain unknown. The artist was not always so tempted; sometimes he sold himself to a patron, but there were not many of them, and so the artist worked for himself, hoping at best that a limited cultured class would recognise him: to-day he must sing to a deaf public, and so is tempted to bray. It is therefore in science and statesmanship that the romantic quality of the future will be found. Romance is a maligned word, debased to fit any calf-love; romance is pinkish, or bluish, tender, feeble, and ends in orange blossom, or, as the case may be, tears by the side of mother's grave. That is the romance of the provincial touring company. True romance is virile, generous, and its voice is as that of the trumpet. Romance is the wage of the watcher, who with ever-open eyes scans the boundless air in eternal expectation that a thing unknown will appear. Romance is the quest of the unknown thing; it is Don Quixote riding Rozinante, Vasco da Gama for the first time passing the Cape; romance is every little boy who dug in the back garden in the hope of reaching the antipodes. For the romantic goal is always on the other side of the hill; everlastingly we seek it in love, for the spirit of the loved thing is on the other side of the hill, because, more exactly, what we seek is on the other side of ourselves.

In our modern world it is possible to lead the romantic life, even though the equator and the poles be accessible to the touring agencies, even though most loves be contracts, for we live in times of disturbance, where war, international and civil holds its sway, where democracies stir, where men are exalted and abased. All times, no doubt, were stirring, and after the fall of the Roman Empire, they followed almost everywhere the same course. After the invasion of the barbarians, romance fell into the hands of the rough knights, who established order by the sword; it passed to the more spiritual knights, who went forth on the Crusade; then the kings dominated the knights, creating States, while the citizens raised their banners and exacted equality with kings; the age of exploration came, the triumph of the merchant in India, Virginia, Hudson's Bay; wealth arose, an ambitious foe of royal and aristocratic power. Then came the revolutions, the American, the French, the European struggle of 1848, the grand battle against slavery, culminating in the United States. That was romance, all that excitement, ambition, achievement, carrying its men high. If citizen slays aristocrat, if rich man slays labour, now labour may slay rich man. Divisions of blood have gone and every day fall lower, as the Portuguese, the Chinese, the Russians set up republican states where no blood is blue. That is not the end, for the modern division is economic, and the romance of mankind will be the establishment of states where strife will kill strife, where tolerance if not justice can reign, where discontent will give way to a content not ignoble.

In the nineteenth and twentieth centuries many romantic lives have been led; startling persons have risen like meteors, and a few still burn like suns. Men like Cecil Rhodes, like Mr Lloyd George, like President Carranza, Mr Hearst, Mr Leiter, Mr Rockefeller, Prince Kropotkin, have lived startling lives of contest and desire. In these movements still obscure, where labour will array itself against wealth, where hideous, tyrannic things will be done in the name of liberty, where hatred will smooth the path to love, I think there will be extraordinary careers because nothing is impossible to men, and a few things may become possible to women. Many say too lightly that opportunity is not as great as under Elizabeth; they forget, that if the arts are sick, other careers are open; while one man could expect coronation by Elizabeth, many can now aim at the high crown of the love or hatred of Demos. Republics, too, can have their Rasputins.

The future of genius lies with science and the State, because the State has effected a corner in power and romance. For art and letters there is little hope in a growingly mechanical civilisation, because the modern powerful depend upon the mob and not upon each other; therefore, as Napoleon said, they must be a little like the mob—be the super-mob. In their view, as in the view of those who follow them, art cannot rival money and domination. The mob hates the arts whenever they rise high, for the arts can be felt, but not understood; at other times it scorns them. Therefore, the arts must suffer from the atmosphere of indifference they must breathe. They will not vanish, for mankind needs always to express itself, its aspiration, its content, its discontent; those three can be expressed only in the arts. But this does not mean that the arts can aspire to thrones or be worthy of them; as science and the State dwarf them, they must become little stimulants, sing little songs that will less and less be heard amid the roar of the spinning world.

W. L. George – A Concise Bibliography

Engines of Social Progress (1907)
France in the Twentieth Century (1908)
Labour and Housing at Port Sunlight (1909)
A Bed of Roses (1911)
City of Light: A Novel of Modern Paris (1912)
Woman and To-morrow (1913)
Israel Kalisch (1913) (In the USA as 'Until the Day Break')
The Making of an Englishman (1914) (Reissued in 1916 as 'The Little Beloved')
The Second Blooming (1914)
Dramatic Actualities (1914)
Olga Nazimov & Other Stories (1915)
Anatole France (1915)
The Intelligence of Woman (1916)
The Strangers' Wedding, Or the Comedy of a Romantic (1916)
A Novelist on Novels (1918) (In the USA as 'Literary Chapters')
Blind Alley (1919)
Eddies of the Day (1919)
Caliban (1920)

The Confession of Ursula Trent (1921) (In the USA as 'Ursula Trent')
A London Mosaic (1921) with illustrations Philippe Forbes-Robertson.
Hail Columbia! Random Impressions of A Conservative English Radical (1921)
The Stiff Lip (1922) (In the USA as 'Her Unwelcome Husband' 1922. Reissued as 'One of the Guilty' 1923)
The Triumph of Gallio (1924)
The Story of Woman (1925)
Historic Lovers (1925)
Children of the Morning (1926)
Gifts of Sheba (1926)
The Ordeal of Monica Mary (1927)
The Selected Short Stories of W. L. George (1927)